AF480690

Confessions
Of the Preacher's
Naughty Daughter

Carnality, Lust, and a Lifetime of Stories

Confessions
Of the Preacher's
Naughty Daughter

Carnality, Lust, and a Lifetime of Stories

Scarlett C. Rose

Words to Ponder Publishing Company, LLC
Chagrin Falls, Ohio

Copyright © 2026 by Scarlett C. Rose
All rights reserved.
No part of this book may be reproduced, stored in a retrieval system, or transmitted in any form or by any means—electronic, mechanical, photocopying, recording, scanning, or otherwise—without prior written permission from the publisher, except for brief quotations used in reviews or scholarly works.
This is a work of nonfiction based on the author's recollections and experiences. Certain names, identifying characteristics, and details have been changed to protect the privacy of individuals. Some scenes may be reconstructed from memory. Any resemblance to persons living or dead other than those clearly identified is coincidental. While every effort has been made to ensure the accuracy of the information in this book, the author and publisher assume no responsibility for errors or omissions, or for damages resulting from the use of the information contained herein.
ISBN (eBook): 979-8-89664-022-6
ISBN (Trade Paperback): 979-8-89664-023-3
ISBN (Hardcover): 979-8-89664-024-0
LCCN: 2026937503

Published by
Words to Ponder Publishing Company, LLC
Chagrin Falls, Ohio
www.wordstoponderpublishing.com
For information about permissions, translations, or special editions, contact:
Contact@florenza.org
Cover design by: Words to Ponder Publishing Company, LLC
Printed in the United States of America
First Edition
10 9 8 7 6 5 4 3 2 1

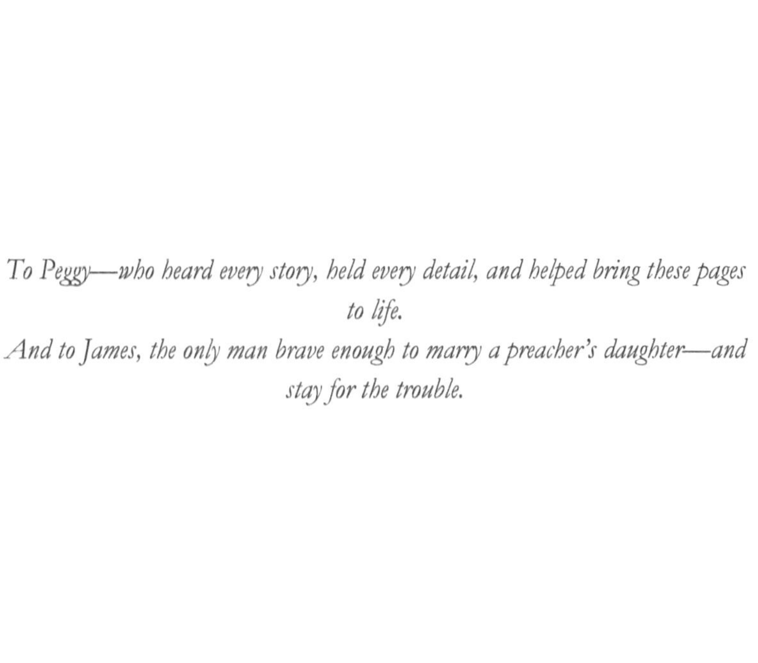

To Peggy—who heard every story, held every detail, and helped bring these pages to life.
And to James, the only man brave enough to marry a preacher's daughter—and stay for the trouble.

"For everything there is a season."
— Ecclesiastes 3:1

Contents

I, Scarlett, do solemnly swear—
not to tell the safe truth.

Everything you're about to read happened.
Every choice. Every scene. Every line I crossed.

Some details are softened.
Not because I'm ashamed.
Because some truths burn hotter than paper.

If you came looking for repentance,
you picked up the wrong book.

I'm not here to be corrected.
I'm here to be accurate.

I made my choices early.
Loudly.
On purpose.

Some of them will make you uncomfortable.
Good.

Shame only has power when you hide from it.
I never hid.

I learned to carry it like a blade and keep walking.

I am the Preacher's Naughty Daughter.

And if you keep reading,
don't pretend curiosity didn't bring you here.

— Scarlett

ACT I: AWAKENING

CONFESSIONS OF AWAKENING

They say every child wants attention.

That's not entirely true.

 Some of us want reaction.

 Attention is polite applause.

Reaction is the sharp inhale when a hymn goes off-key.

The whisper behind you.

The look your mother gives when she knows you did it on purpose.

 I learned early that chaos answers when you call it.

 It hums.

It crackles.

It gathers people before they realize they've leaned closer.

 I wasn't trying to be wicked.

I was trying to feel something bigger than "good girl."

 Once I realized I could tilt a room with a single word—

I stopped waiting for permission.

 That's the problem with discovery.

Once you know the room will move when you touch it,

you never go back to sitting still.

 You don't fall asleep after that.

 — Scarlett

CHAPTER ONE

Everyone thought I was the nicest, sweetest, most angelic child in the church.

They were wrong.

I was red-haired, freckle-faced, precocious, and dangerously inventive—the kind of preacher's daughter people pretend they don't know, then whisper about in the parking lot like a prayer request.

Mommy marched me to Sunday school every week in our little Midwestern town. I danced on cue, sang on pitch, sat pretty on the front pew, nodded during Daddy's sermons, and curtsied for the parishioners.

My parents were very proud.

Until they weren't.

By the tender age of three, I had become a holy terror in Shirley Temple curls.

While Mommy sang in the choir, I pinched my baby brother just hard enough to make him scream in harmony with the organ. I interrupted sermons with a thunderous "Amen!" when Daddy least expected it. I crawled under pews and switched shoes for sport—high heels two rows back replaced with little Buster Brown saddle shoes.

When service ended, I stood on the pew and watched confusion bloom like a revival meeting, smiling sweetly while grown adults searched for their dignity and their footwear.

That was my first religion: reaction.

Daddy earned a preacher's pittance, yet somehow, I maintained a very healthy piggy bank.

The mystery unraveled when Mommy questioned the church ladies.

Apparently, I had been stationed at the exit, opening my tiny purse and asked each departing parishioner for "offering money for my poor daddy."

They gave generously.

Mommy later found the stash behind my stuffed animals.

An old-fashioned spanking followed.

Did it deter me?

Absolutely not.

A few welts was a small price for profit.

By four, the church teenagers realized I was useful. After Sunday service, they stationed me in the front seat while they conducted very enthusiastic fellowship in the back.

I earned a quarter each night by shouting warnings when adults entered the parking lot.

The couples would bolt upright—hymnals practically materializing in their hands.

From the front seat, I listened.

The giggles.

The whispers.

The sharp hush when a door slammed.

I didn't have language for what I was hearing yet.

But I noticed what it did to people.

How it made them careless.

How it made them brave.

How it made them reckless.

And I remembered.

On Tuesday mornings, Mommy took me to Bible study at the Baptist preacher's house. While the mothers discussed scripture in the living room, we children were sealed in the den behind a closed door.

I turned it into rehearsal.

I copied what I'd seen, the way children do—too confident, too curious, too sure the room belonged to me.

I recruited boys old enough to follow instructions and young enough not to question them.

Bathrooms.

Bedrooms.

Closets when privacy could be negotiated.

Some boys were more dedicated students than others.

I called them my good boys.

When kindergarten began, I expanded operations, playground bushes, storage rooms, any place that felt like a secret.

At six, I was suspended for chasing a new fourth-grade boy across the playground, tackling him, straddling him, ripping the buttons from his shirt, and kissing him into stunned silence.

The other boys immediately formed a line.

One of them was Gary—cute, attentive, easily persuaded.

He asked me to be his girlfriend.

I said yes.

On one condition.

A ring.

The next day he arrived with a diamond ring on a chain.

I wore it proudly for nearly a month before Mommy noticed.

"Scarlett Rose! What are you doing with a diamond ring?"

Turns out Gary's grandmother was missing her late husband's engagement ring.

We were separated like star-crossed lovers and detained during recess for months.

No one seemed particularly concerned with why I wanted it.

Only that I had taken it.

Back at church, I resumed my angelic face. I nodded at the right moments and said "Amen" on cue.

But during hymns, all hell broke loose.

I screeched off-key just to rattle my parents. When Mommy sang solos, I pinched my baby brother to sabotage her high notes or made faces until she forgot the lyrics.

Daddy eventually summoned me to sit on the stage beside him during sermons.

Big mistake.

I trimmed my bangs with fingernail clippers mid-sermon. I hiked my dress high enough to flash lace. I mimicked Daddy's gestures. I yawned theatrically for effect.

Sometimes Daddy stopped preaching altogether and spanked me right there on the stage.

It hurt.

The congregation never knew where to look.

I liked that part too.

Silence bored me.

Consequences were just noise.

Even then, my rebellion wasn't budding—it was already blooming.

They thought I was playing.

I wasn't.

CHAPTER TWO

When I was seven, Daddy joined the military.

Before we moved, my parents sat me down and explained that military church was formal. Quiet. Respectful. If I embarrassed Daddy, he could lose his job.

I didn't want us to be poor again.

So, I behaved.

For almost an entire year.

(Which, frankly, deserves recognition.)

At Daddy's first post, we joined a downtown ministry that served people in the red-light district—drug addicts, prostitutes, men who looked like they hadn't slept in days.

It was off-limits to enlisted soldiers.

Which made it irresistible.

Since no babysitter would take me—and I couldn't be trusted anyway—I went along every weekend.

While Mommy and Daddy counseled people in the back office, I ran the front.

Coffee. Sandwiches. Conversation.

I told dramatic stories about my "bad girl" past to wide-eyed adults.

They told me about their teenage rebellions.

I listened closely.

I didn't care much about their regret.

I cared about the spark.

The way their eyes changed when they stopped pretending.

But the prostitutes—

they were different.

Shiny skirts. Wild makeup. High heels that clicked like punctuation.

They talked about their boyfriends constantly.

I watched them the way other girls watched princesses.

They didn't look ashamed.

They looked chosen.

At least from where I stood.

That's when I decided I wanted to be a prostitute when I grew up.

Not for the money.

For the boyfriends.

For the kind of attention that didn't have to disguise itself as holiness.

A few of the regulars even wrote a song for me—a secret song I was never supposed to sing in front of my parents.

I performed it anyway.

And I performed it beautifully.

I wish I was a fascinating lady
With a past that was fast
And a future that looks shady
In a little white house
With a little red light
And once a month
I'd take a short vacation
Just to drive my customers wild…
I wish I was a fascinating lady
Instead of a minister's child.

At the end, I blew kisses.

They applauded.

And something settled into place.

It wasn't corruption.

It wasn't innocence.

It was recognition.

CHAPTER THREE

Austin's working girls helped me rewrite the last line of "I'm a Little Teapot."

I'd belt it out in a dramatic voice —

"Sock it to me, baby! Let it all hang out!"

Then I'd turn around, hike up my dress, and wiggle for the audience.

I wasn't trying to scandalize anyone.

I was performing.

Underneath were my baby sister's pink ruffled diaper covers.

I wore them like costume pieces — borrowed glamour from women who seemed to command rooms without asking permission.

A few years later, at our next duty station, the military kids were bused to an intermediate school filled mostly with Spanish-speaking students.

I learned Spanish quickly.

Not because I loved language.

Because I refused to be talked about without knowing what was being said.

When the boys heard I liked to make out, I became popular.

The girls were unimpressed.

One afternoon during recess, I stood in the center of a loose circle of boys who acted as if I'd invented oxygen.

One of them asked if I was a virgin.

I paused.

The only place I'd heard that word was in church — Holy Mother Mary, virgin, baby Jesus.

I had never had a baby.

So I said no.

I answered with certainty.

Understanding had nothing to do with it.

By lunch, I was a rumor.

By dismissal, I was a headline.

The boys lined up to be my boyfriend.

I moved through them quickly — not because I grasped the implications, but because I liked what happened when they competed.

It changed the air.

A teacher eventually pulled me aside and explained what the word meant.

It didn't matter.

Reputations travel faster than corrections.

Mine stayed.

For the next two years, older boys began circling.

I didn't understand the danger.

I understood the shift in power.

And at that age,

that felt like enough.

CHAPTER FOUR

The military post closed, so we moved to a massive training base filled with new recruits—mostly late teens and early twenties.

I wasn't yet fourteen.

In Texas, when my parents left at night for church meetings and choir practice, I babysat my brother and sister.

The second their taillights disappeared, boys knocked at the back door.

It wasn't chaos.

It was a schedule.

No overlaps.

No surprises.

No one stepping on anyone else's time slot.

I looked forward to it every week.

Not the romance.

The electricity.

At the new post, Daddy's job changed.

The nighttime church meetings vanished.

So did my window.

I didn't panic.

I adjusted.

I started babysitting for young officers' families and priced myself just low enough to stay fully booked.

It looked helpful.

It looked responsible.

It wasn't.

That was my first real system.

CHAPTER FIVE

School started, and there were plenty of boys—but none interesting enough lived on post.

Daddy's job was at the military hospital chapel. No Sunday school. No youth programs.

So my parents dropped us at a larger family chapel in an area called the Triangle.

It was named for geography.

Three sides of the chapel and mess hall were surrounded by rows of soldier barracks.

I walked into that first service and saw pew after pew of short-haired men sitting in street clothes.

Still.

Waiting.

After the service, one of them slipped me the number to the main desk at his barracks.

He'd be on duty the next night.

I'd be babysitting.

I called.

I flirted.

I repeated the process every night I worked, dialing whatever barracks desk was listed and talking to whoever answered.

I later learned the men on desk duty were usually there for disciplinary reasons.

Troublemakers.

Which meant they were bored.

And boredom makes people talk.

That's when I realized I needed privacy.

I began inviting them to meet me at the Triangle chapel on Sundays.

They'd sit on a bench in the prayer garden behind the building.

After the choir sang, I'd slip out before the sermon and join them.

We talked.

Sometimes that was all.

We kissed if the garden was empty.

Just before noon, I'd rush back into the chapel, flushed and composed, collect my siblings, and greet my parents like nothing had happened.

That was when it started to feel effortless.

Like the room had finally learned its cues.

CHAPTER SIX

You'd think I would have been satisfied.

I wasn't.

Satisfied was never the point.

When I called the barracks, the GIs would ask my name.

I introduced myself as George.

Short. Safe. Male.

The name stuck.

Around the Triangle, George became a rumor before he became a person.

If I wanted someone in my regular rotation, I gave him my home phone number and told him to ask for George.

I was quick to answer.

Sometimes my parents were quicker.

They'd answer the phone, look around the room, and ask aloud who George was.

I'd shrug and say maybe he used to have this number.

They accepted it.

Now fifteen, I had a rotating cast of men — but routine dulls.

And dull bores me.

I wanted escalation.

So I refined it.

I started asking who had access to a car.

If they didn't, they were out.

Mobility mattered.

I needed men who could reach officers' housing.

If they qualified, I'd have them bring a couple of friends, knock softly at my bedroom window after midnight, and drive off post.

Sneaking out became standard.

Often, I invited a girl from school to spend the night so I wouldn't be the only one with something to lose.

The sleepovers I enjoyed most were with other preacher's daughters — the kind whose fathers were guest speakers at our church the next morning.

Their parents believed I was the model minister's child.
I let them.

Midnight calls were made.
Arrangements were understood.

Two preacher's daughters in one car carried its own mythology.

They left with stories.
We left with momentum.

ACT II: ESCALATION

CONFESSION OF ESCALATION

There's a moment when curiosity stops being accidental
and becomes intentional.

I had already learned rooms would shift if I applied pressure.

So I leaned harder.

Phone calls after midnight.

A name that wasn't mine.

Windows that opened from the inside.

Men who understood the risk — and came anyway.

You're about to read things that didn't simply happen.

I arranged them.

Escalation wasn't chaos.

It was design.

Older.

Riskier.

More precise.

I liked the calculation.

How many lies could hold at once?

How far could I move before someone noticed?

You might think this is where I should have stopped.

It isn't.

Because once you realize you can survive the first boundary,
you stop asking whether you should cross the next one.

You just measure the distance.

— Scarlett

CHAPTER SEVEN

School was a different matter.

I landed in the first year of racial integration in the southern states. Military kids got bussed straight into the city — into a school filled with Black students that used to be a recreation center. It even had a swimming pool.

I thought that was the coolest thing I'd ever heard.

Then the first day happened.

Police escorted our bus through armed gates while protesters waved signs telling us to go home.

Just like that, the swimming pool lost its shine.

It was tense.

It was loud.

It was historic whether we liked it or not.

I've never had trouble inserting myself into a room.

Within weeks, girls were plaiting my long red hair each morning. I learned how to code-switch before I knew there was a term for it.

I adapted.

I always do.

And yes — I still got into trouble.

I spent plenty of afternoons bent over touching my toes while the vice principal paddled discipline into me.

Each crack of wood against skin didn't humble me.

It instructed me.

It taught me where the line was — and how to step around it next time.

Eventually I caught the eye of the team's star player — tall, dark, handsome, with an afro that deserved its own introduction.

He and his friends let me orbit their circle.

They shielded me from a teacher whose eyes lingered too long. From another who called me immoral just for breathing too confidently.

From jealous girls who didn't appreciate my popularity crossing lines they thought were permanent.

And then the lines crossed back.

One afternoon near the boys' locker room, a white football player stepped in front of me.

He said I loved Black boys.

The way he said it made the hallway smaller.

He grabbed me — hard enough to bruise — and shoved me through the locker room door.

His friends were already inside.

I'm not dressing this up.

They violated me.

They hurled slurs like they were trying to brand me with them.

Here's what unsettles people:

I didn't scream.

I didn't freeze.

I didn't give them what they wanted.

There was a knock.

A coach's voice cut through the noise.

Practice.

They scattered.

Boys remembering consequences.

I pulled my clothes straight.

Smoothed my hair with hands that trembled — but only once the door was closed.

I walked out like I had somewhere important to be.

I got on the bus.

I told no one.

I wasn't ashamed.

I wasn't broken.

And I wasn't going to hand them the power to narrate me.
Not on that base.
Not in that climate.
Not with my father's name stitched onto a uniform.
So I chose something else.
If I was going to be seen,
it would be on my terms.

CHAPTER EIGHT

That summer Daddy took the family to California so he could earn his Doctorate in Theology.

We landed in a neighborhood thick with hippies and incense.

I felt instantly at home.

I enrolled in summer school — poetry and typing.

Nobody wore shoes.

The Grateful Dead played during class like background scripture.

The teachers smoked weed with the students before lectures and called it "expanding consciousness."

It was 1974 — the age of freedom — and I slipped into it like it had been waiting for me.

Beads.

Bell-bottoms.

Bare feet.

Free love without the church bulletin.

Life was good.

Then I started seeing a familiar face hovering outside school grounds.

One of my former GIs.

He lingered like unfinished business.

A few days later, while we were visiting a museum downtown, he walked straight up to Daddy and announced that God had told him to marry me.

I almost choked.

Daddy didn't blink.

"Well son, when God tells me that my fifteen-year-old daughter is to marry you, I'll look you up. Until then, don't go anywhere near her."

Daddy called the young man's commander and reported him AWOL — Absent Without Leave.

Translation:

God may have told you to marry me,

but the Army was about to discipline you.

Just like that.

That had been my first proposal.

I laughed for days.

California ended.

We moved back home.

The GIs resumed rotation for about another year — business as usual — until one evening my parents sat me down with faces so serious I thought someone had died.

They asked if I knew a girl named Georgia.

Georgia?

Apparently, Georgia had been enticing soldiers to sneak out of the barracks after lights out.

A few had been caught.

They'd confessed to their commanding officers.

Word had reached the General.

He was furious.

They knew Georgia was an officer's daughter.

They knew she lived on base.

They knew she called the barracks late at night.

And — this was new information — she had even been smuggled into the barracks from time to time.

I kept my face innocent.

Halo intact.

"I don't know a Georgia," I said. "Or anyone who'd sin so openly. All of my friends are like me. Wholesome."

My parents nodded, relieved.

They had no idea they were sitting across from Georgia.

If not for their blinders, they might have noticed.

The cat at their kitchen table wasn't housebroken.
She was calculating.
Georgia wasn't roaming the barracks.
She was passing the butter.
I had to fight the urge to take a bow.
My reputation was expanding.
And I liked knowing it had outgrown the room.

CHAPTER NINE

One dark, storm-heavy night, I heard the familiar tap at my window.

I hadn't invited anyone.

Curiosity won.

I lifted the blinds and looked down to see a younger girl and her little brother standing in the rain.

I opened the back door and pulled them inside without a word.

The General's children.

Yes.

That General.

The one hunting George.

They'd been disciplined that evening and decided they'd had enough.

They wanted to run away.

Of course they did.

And of course they came to me.

They had relatives in town.

That was the plan.

I called the barracks and convinced some unsuspecting GI to come get us.

I told him it was urgent.

I always knew how to make things sound urgent.

I was wearing a mini nightdress and fuzzy pink slippers.

The children were in pajamas and robes.

We looked like a bedtime mutiny.

What I didn't know was that the General's wife had already alerted him the children were missing.

He issued an APB — All-Points Bulletin — on every vehicle entering and leaving the base.

Once we were off post, the children admitted they didn't actually know where their relatives lived.

Details.

We turned around.

At the security gate, the military police stopped the car.

Flashlights.

Questions.

Faces hardening.

We were escorted into the station to "await our fates."

The General arrived furious.

Boots striking concrete.

Voice already raised.

Guess which Chaplain they called to keep the room from detonating.

My father.

He walked into the military police hut and stopped.

There I was — perched on a desk in my nightdress, legs swinging, the picture of terrible judgment.

The room went quiet.

The General shouted.

The GI paled when he was told charges were coming.

For the first time in a long time, I felt something close to clarity.

I prayed.

It didn't change anything.

A few weeks later, my father received orders.

Europe.

Immediate transfer.

The GI was discharged.

My good deed had collateral damage.

Turns out, when you volunteer to be the scandal,

you don't control the blast radius.

I hadn't meant to take anyone down with me.

But I hadn't promised not to, either.

CHAPTER TEN

Would that have been the end of George?

Oh no.

The first thing my parents did when we reached Europe was sit me down and give me an ultimatum.

Either I surrendered my rebellious lifestyle —

or my father would surrender his calling.

As a Chaplain, he said he couldn't counsel other families if he couldn't manage his own daughter.

He couldn't preach about Christ and moral example while I was turning barracks into brothels.

To drive the point home, they had me kneel at the altar in their bedroom.

Yes.

They had an altar in their bedroom.

I was told to ask God's forgiveness.

To cry.

To repent.

To promise I would never return to that lifestyle again.

I didn't cry.

But I said every word they needed to hear.

When you grow up in a preacher's house, you learn early how to deliver conviction on cue.

They dismissed me to bed.

Crisis managed.

People have always been drawn to me.

Not because I was good.

Because I was interesting.

When I told stories, crowds formed.

I had timing.

Humor.

Just enough detail to make people lean forward.

I could turn a minor inconvenience into something cinematic.

I could make shame look like style.

It was a skill.

My parents had one too.

As we traveled through Europe, they'd walk up to total strangers — in cafés, train stations, markets — and begin conversations that ended with Jesus.

I used to joke that they ambushed people.

But I watched.

They drew people in.

Held them there.

Made them feel seen.

I studied that.

I was never drawn to the well-behaved.

I liked the ones who didn't fit — hippies, addicts, unwed mothers, prostitutes, the destitute.

The ones who carried stories like exposed nerves.

I read everything I could find about lives like theirs.

Redemption memoirs.

Confessions.

Downfalls.

But if I'm honest?

I was more fascinated by who they were before the reform.

When I found someone intriguing, I did what my parents did.

I walked straight up and started talking.

Conversations lasted for hours.

They introduced me to their friends.

I asked questions no one else asked.

Why this life?

What are you really afraid of?

What do you want that you won't admit out loud?

I stored their answers.

At dinner, my parents discussed counseling sessions openly — details, dilemmas, strategies.

I absorbed everything.

Their cadence.

Their patience.

Their leverage.

I began applying it.

Not because I felt holy.

Because I understood people.

If someone was hurting, misunderstood, anxious, lost — I moved toward them.

I took on their problems like equations.

I researched.

I advised.

I listened.

My friends called them my projects.

My parents called them my ministries.

They wanted to save souls from damnation.

I stood beside the fire.

Not to extinguish it —

but to see who stepped closer.

CHAPTER ELEVEN

What started as me chasing people turned into people chasing me.

They called me an empath.
Said light came off my face.
Said the broken felt safe around me.
I never corrected them.
New post.
New school.
New slate.
No GIs.
At least not immediately.
There was one boy my age who lived nearby.
David.
Football player.
A streak of trouble in him.
He did what I wanted.
When I wanted.
That was sufficient.
The chapel was smaller now.
Daddy had been reassigned.
His reports had followed him.
We were being watched.
Two GIs attended regularly.
One short and red-haired.
One tall and long-limbed.
Chapel was the only place I was allowed near them.
Which made it perfect.

Then one Sunday, the short one approached Daddy and declared God had told him to marry me.

Daddy gave his speech.

I laughed.

Proposal number two.

The convention invitation came weeks later.

Daddy was to preach at another installation.

He invited the tall GI to travel with us.

Snowstorm.

Mountain road.

I chose the middle seat.

I didn't need to say much.

I never did.

The afternoon felt victorious.

The evening felt inevitable.

We arrived late.

Testimonies were already underway.

Stories of salvation.

Of redemption.

Of souls rescued from themselves.

We slipped in near the pulpit.

Then the man speaking stopped mid-sentence.

Pointed.

At me.

"That's George!" he shouted.

"That's the girl I told you about!

She invited me to chapel one morning.

I went looking for her, heard the sermon, and gave my life to Christ!

George led me to the Lord!"

The room erupted.

Hands raised.

Voices lifted.

Hallelujahs.

Everyone was celebrating.

Except my parents.

Their faces went still.

Not angry.

Still.

IT. WAS. OVER.

For the next hour I sat through Daddy's sermon knowing I had just become Exhibit A.

Proof that chaos could evangelize.

The drive home was silent.

The GI stared out the window as if proximity might damn him.

That stung more than I expected.

Snow fell thicker as we climbed the mountain pass.

Mom told us to pray.

Daddy hit black ice.

The car spun.

The guardrail rushed toward us.

Mom screamed Jesus' name.

And in that split second, I understood something:

I had been flirting with fire.

And fire does not negotiate.

The car stopped.

Facing headlights.

Still alive.

For now.

CHAPTER TWELVE

We reached home in the early hours of the morning.

I was summoned immediately.

Their bedroom altar had made the move to Europe.

Of course it had.

I knelt.

Again.

They repeated the lecture from months earlier — only this time it carried less fear and more fury.

I tried to soften the blow.

"At least something good came from it," I said. "He led hundreds of people to Christ after that."

Wrong move.

I had never seen them this angry.

They spanked me.

Harder this time.

Called me a liar.

A bad influence.

A conniving manipulator.

The words landed heavier than the blows.

Then I was back at the altar.

Repent.

Cry.

Ask forgiveness.

I knew they were right about one thing.

I could move a room.

So I did what I always did.

I moved them.

I said the right words.

Shed no tears.

I was already on lockdown.

Now it tightened.

Home directly after school.

No phone.

No detours.

A monastery would have felt freer.

But confinement is just architecture.

In my mind, I revised my strategy.

Pranks?

Fine.

Flirting?

Fine.

Experimenting?

Containable.

Trouble — but only the kind I could outrun.

Men were off limits.

For now.

Public scandal was off limits too.

I would not get caught again.

I moved from the back of the bus to the front.

Optics matter.

I joined the Cross Country team so I'd have a legitimate excuse to stay after school.

Five miles a day.

Adidas laced tight.

I ran behind beautifully muscled boys in short shorts and let them enjoy being admired.

They thought I was reforming.

I was studying.

For once, I wasn't the headline.

I was the editor.

CHAPTER THIRTEEN

David and I carried reputations at school and church, but at home we met like it was training.

It wasn't romance.

It wasn't destiny.

It was competition.

One evening after cross-country, I came home to an empty apartment.

Church night.

I ran a bath and left the lights off.

Moonlight slipped across the tile.

Lavender steam gathered near the ceiling.

I sank beneath the bubbles and stretched, my red hair fanning out like something fallen from its halo.

The door opened.

David stepped in, silent, still warm from football drills.

He pulled his shirt over his head without looking at me.

The moon cut across his shoulders and made him look carved instead of grown.

When he stepped into the tub, the water shifted around him like it had been expecting him.

We didn't talk.

There wasn't anything to negotiate.

It was heat.

Breath.

Familiar ground.

He left the way he entered — steady, unremarkable — as if nothing had shifted at all.

That night, I felt untouchable.

——— 🍎 ———

A few weeks later, a new girl boarded the bus for the long ride
to school.

She carried herself small, like she was apologizing for taking up
space.

I slid over before anyone else could claim the seat.

By the time we reached campus, I knew enough.

Selena.

Two years younger.

Soft voice.

Beautiful in a way that hadn't been weaponized yet.

I decided we were friends.

"I like you," I told her.

"Stay close."

She smiled with relief.

She didn't realize she'd been enlisted.

Selena balanced me.

Stand me beside her and I looked almost harmless.

I showed her how to hold eye contact a beat too long.

How to tilt her chin.

How to step back before a boy realized he'd leaned forward.

We practiced wherever attention gathered — German boys, GIs
in town, whoever blushed first.

Advance.

Retreat.

Leave them unsure.

Sports gave us mobility.

Cross-country.

Track.

Theater trips across bases in Europe.

Long bus rides thick with boredom.

Hotels.

Hallways.

Doors that shut easily.

I watched how rooms worked.

Confidence opened them.

Access decided who stayed.

Trust made everything simpler.

Teachers believed me.

I gave them no reason not to.

I assigned rooms.

Organized excursions.

Arranged seating charts.

I moved people like pieces that didn't know they were on a board.

They called it leadership.

I called it structure.

On the troop train to East Berlin, we were ordered to keep curtains closed and faces away from the glass.

Guards and wire flashed by in the dark.

I pulled the curtain back anyway.

One girl stood watch.

Another stalled in the aisle.

By the time security passed, we were composed again — cards in hand, innocence arranged.

The coach stationed himself outside our compartment for the rest of the ride.

I took that as acknowledgment.

Berlin split the world into visible lines — East and West, free and watched.

After Selena won her race, we celebrated badly.

Wine we weren't meant to have.

A wrong subway platform that delivered us briefly to the wrong side of the border.

Real fear tastes metallic.

We corrected course.

I memorized the sensation.

Risk accelerates everything.

By senior year, I set a goal.

No one in our class of fifty-four would graduate untouched.

It started as a joke.

Then it didn't.

I recruited strategically — confident boys who could steady awkward ones.

I matched temperaments.

Nudged shy girls toward curiosity.

Chose room assignments carefully on trips.

I told myself I was helping.

One officer's son stiffened whenever a girl brushed his hand.

I took him to a German brothel, stood nearby while he studied the menu like a final exam, paid the fee, and waited outside.

He walked out different.

Straighter.

Another boy stalled with his girlfriend on a sleeper train to Italy.

I adjusted the atmosphere, corrected the tension, then stepped aside.

I wasn't corrupting anyone.

I was clearing friction.

When only one holdout remained — an officer's daughter too insulated for anyone to approach — I arranged a quiet agreement with a GI.

Dinners first.
An understanding.
Compensation after.
It happened.
No spectacle.
I marked it done and moved on.
I never became the fantasy I once imagined as a child.
But I understood logistics.
Leverage.
And that most people need permission more than instruction.

If my parents believed they were saving souls,
I was opening doors.
They spoke about repentance.
I organized experience.
The unsettling part wasn't what I did.
It was how certain I was that I was right.

CHAPTER FOURTEEN

On another troop train trip from Berlin, I decided the team needed something to remember me by.

They were exhausted.

Cross-country legs heavy.

Spirits flat.

I wasn't.

I pulled a few runners into a tight circle and reached into my duffel bag.

Out came a clean pair of red lace panties.

Not subtle.

I've never been subtle.

With a black Sharpie, I wrote across the front:

Home of So-and-So High School.

On the tag, I added the teacher's daughter's initials.

Details matter.

When we rolled back into the school parking lot that evening, parents crowded the curb, hugging their children and hauling duffel bags into trunks.

While the adults were distracted, three boys slipped off with the merchandise.

Up the flagpole it went — the red lace panties and one of my bright floral bras, padded with paper towels for structure — climbing until they hovered level with the Principal's office window.

By morning, they were flying.

The entire school saw them before he did.

He ordered them taken down in a rage.

But it was already done.

No one asked who was responsible.

They knew.

I didn't create chaos by accident.
I branded it — bright red and flying high.

41

CHAPTER FIFTEEN

At chapel one morning — yes, I still went, still sat on the front pew, still said "Amen" on cue — another GI decided he had received divine revelation.

He told Daddy he had fasted for forty days and that God had instructed him to marry me.

This one was almost impressive.

I hadn't flirted with him.

Had barely spoken to him.

Hadn't even given him my good eye.

Yet there he stood, breathless, announcing destiny.

He had already purchased a ticket for me to return to the States with him after graduation.

Daddy delivered the same speech he'd given the others.

Then he glared at me.

I wasn't sure why.

Later that afternoon, I was summoned — again — to the bedroom altar.

The topic?

Greece.

I had made a small assumption.

I believed distance created immunity.

On a crosswalk near the Acropolis, I locked eyes with a man who looked carved from the same stone as the statues behind him.

I gave him a slow wink.

He tilted his head.

I nodded.

That was it.

Or so I believed.

He appeared in a shop a few minutes later.

Followed us through narrow streets.

Stood beneath our seaside hotel balcony.

Silent.

Waiting.

When Daddy confronted the hotel manager, the explanation came back simple:

The girl invited him.

A look.

A signal.

An agreement.

Apparently, in some places, a wink isn't mischief.

It's permission.

He eventually left.

The conversation did not.

Back in Europe, my parents connected what they saw as a pattern — the proposal, the wink, the history.

Back to the altar.

Back to prayer.

Back to repentance.

I stood there, hands folded.

Life wasn't unfair.

It was cause and effect.

And I was very good at acting surprised.

CHAPTER SIXTEEN

I still sang in the church choir.

Loudly.

Confidently.

Wildly off key.

Everyone knew it.

Everyone laughed.

The altos glared.

The sopranos pleaded.

Eventually, the choir director surrendered and moved me to the men's bass section.

Imagine that.

A red-haired preacher's daughter wedged between bass voices like an administrative error.

They instructed me to mouth the words.

I agreed.

I did not comply.

I couldn't help it.

I'd slip back into full-volume "blending," which sounded less like harmony and more like an alarm system.

This went on for months.

I found it delightful.

No one could silence me.

Or so I believed.

One bright Sunday morning, sunlight poured through the stained-glass windows like it had somewhere important to be.

We stood to sing.

I opened my mouth.

And then—

CRACK.

A sound like wood snapping under pressure.

Half a stained-glass panel tore loose from its frame and dropped straight down.

Toward me.

It struck my shoulder and landed there, upright, as if placed.

If I hadn't been standing there, it would have shattered across the sanctuary floor.

The chapel went still.

No laughter.

Not even mine.

I didn't cry.

I was too startled.

But by the time Daddy began his sermon, my shoulder was throbbing in steady pulses.

After service, he drove me more than an hour to the nearest military hospital.

Broken collarbone.

Sling.

Orders to rest.

On the drive home, Daddy said one thing.

"Scarlett, I believe that was an Act of God."

He paused.

"Perhaps indicating you should no longer sing in the choir."

And just like that, my musical career ended.

I can't say I repented.

But I did stop singing.

Even I recognize when something falls directly on me.

CHAPTER SEVENTEEN

After graduation, Daddy received orders to attend school back in the South.

My parents decided I would live at home.

Dorm life, they explained, required trust.

I had not accumulated enough of it.

I enrolled at a local community college and did what I've always done best —

recalibrated.

New zip code.

New reputation.

New variables.

At eighteen, I still couldn't drive.

Europe hadn't required parallel parking.

My parents hired another student with a similar class schedule to shuttle me to campus.

A few months in, her father died.

She picked up a job to help with tuition and asked if I wanted in.

That's how I joined the California Collar Sewers' Union.

Yes.

That was real.

We attached collars to name-brand t-shirts as they rolled toward us in bundles of twelve.

Stamp ID.

Align collar.

Feed fabric into the machine.

Press the knee lever.

The lever released a guillotine blade.

On my first night off probation, the woman beside me screamed — sharp, wrong — and held up her hand.

The tip of her finger was gone.

After that, my foot hesitated before every cut.

I checked the fabric.

Then checked it again.

My fingers never drifted near the blade.

The factory noticed.

The next night my bundles came back down the belt, tagged for correction.

Every one of them.

My ID stamped neatly like proof.

Collars too tight.

Collars slipping toward the shoulder.

Some small enough to choke a doll.

Others wide enough to sag.

Most landed in discard.

Caution was expensive.

The women made that clear.

Production slowed around me.

Conversations stopped when I passed.

I wasn't the new girl anymore.

I was the delay.

Eventually a woman approached as "the representative."

"If you don't resign tonight," she said calmly, "we'll handle it after shift."

I believed her.

Daddy picked me up twenty minutes later.

My ride to school declined further involvement in my transportation future.

Daddy announced he would teach me himself.

I passed the driving test on my third attempt.

I was not skilled at reversing, aligning, estimating space, or trusting mirrors.

But the state of California approved me anyway.

The first morning I drove Daddy's woody station wagon to campus, I arrived early enough to claim a pull-through spot with no cars on either side.

Planning matters.

After class, I eased out flawlessly, relocated to a central lot, and wedged myself between two sports cars that looked expensive enough to take offense.

When I reversed, I felt resistance.

Then the long metallic scrape of consequence.

I had introduced Daddy's station wagon to the back right quarter panel of a Mercedes.

I left a note.

Name.

Number.

Apology.

Daddy's vehicle showed no visible damage.

I went to lunch.

After my next class across campus, I reversed again.

Contact.

Different car.

Same Mercedes.

Opposite side.

A student approached gently.

"I know whose car that is."

He escorted me to the owner.

The young man pulled a slip of paper from his wallet.

"Your name is Scarlett," he said.

He held up the note I had written that morning.

"You damaged the right side of my graduation Mercedes.

And now you've damaged the left."

He did not smile.

By then a crowd had formed.

Including a reporter from the campus paper.

The following morning, a full-color front-page article featured the wounded Mercedes — and me beside Daddy's woody.

Students were advised to park at a safe distance.

Eventually campus maintenance intervened.

Whether for my safety or theirs remains unclear.

They painted a custom pull-through space.

Added buffer lines.

Installed a sign.

Reserved for Scarlett.

Fame arrives dressed strangely.

This one smelled like hot rubber and embarrassment.

CHAPTER EIGHTEEN

I joined Intervarsity Christian Fellowship to make my parents happy.

I thought it was a sports club.

It wasn't.

It was a Bible study group.

I should have left immediately — but the leader was tall, charismatic, and had the kind of jawline that made Scripture sound competitive.

So I stayed.

I told myself proximity to holiness might recalibrate me.

I attended meetings.

Raised money for missionaries.

Drove across the base before sunrise, skirting the flight line like a pilgrim with good hair and questionable motives.

For a brief stretch, I considered the possibility that I was evolving.

Then there was a knock at our door.

I opened it to find a rumpled, sweating college boy from the fellowship standing on our porch like he'd misplaced both his dignity and his map.

"How did you get here?" I asked.

"Security stopped me at the gate," he said.

"No military decal. I left my car and walked."

He had walked around the entire air base.

Two hours.

For me.

He asked to speak to my father.

Absolutely not.

I stepped into the street and began dismantling whatever fantasy he had built.

"You're an accounting major.
I debate policy for sport.
You're an introvert.
I set off alarms.
You like country music.
I prefer distortion.
You're devout.
I'm… complicated."
I kept talking, certain logic would send him home.
Then he said it.
"God told me…"
And right there — under the afternoon sun — he urinated down his leg.
There are moments when irony stops pretending to be subtle.
This was one of them.
I called my father outside.
The boy delivered his proposal through damp khakis.
Daddy responded with the same speech he'd given the others.
Calm.
Controlled.
Final.
Then he went back inside to finish dinner.
The suitor had a two-hour walk back to his car.
Proposal number four.
I was eighteen.
I never returned to the fellowship.
Not out of conviction.
I simply refused to become someone's testimony illustration.
Daddy finished school.
We moved again.
This time he joined an inspection team.
No permanent congregation.
Which meant sermons directed at me.

Unacceptable.

I suggested he market himself as a guest preacher to surrounding churches.

Pastors need vacations.

Congregations need substitutes.

He loved the idea.

Within weeks, we were church-hopping every Sunday.

New pulpits.

New pews.

New audiences.

And new men.

I told myself I was still negotiating between the angel on my right shoulder and the devil on my left.

The truth?

I preferred managing both.

CHAPTER NINETEEN

One Sunday evening, Daddy preached at a large local church.

After the handshakes and hallelujahs, I drifted toward the back and saw a girl I recognized from post housing.

"Scarlett," I said, offering my hand.

"Priscilla."

She was sitting with a boy who looked like Donnie Osmond's less obedient cousin.

"This is James," she said.

James.

They were heading out for pizza with the youth group and invited me along.

James offered to drive me home afterward.

Pizza with a cute boy?

Yes.

At Pizza Hut, James sat between us.

Painfully shy.

Which made him interesting.

I asked questions.

He answered carefully.

Metal rock.

Muscle cars.

A streak of mischief he didn't advertise.

I leaned closer.

Brushed the hair at the back of his neck.

Let my fingers rest lightly on his knee beneath the table.

He went still.

Good.

That night I told my parents I felt "led" to make that church our new home.

They agreed.

The next Sunday I sat beside Priscilla again.

James between us.

I made sure her parents liked me.

I made sure his parents liked me.

I made sure everyone liked me.

Under the table, my hand found him again.

He jumped.

A small sound escaped him.

I was awake.

Since James was officially courting good Christian Priscilla, I needed a distraction.

Enter Bill — military police, youth group regular.

Not my type.

But stable.

Predictable.

Useful.

I was nineteen and had technically never been on a "real" date.

Bill was respectful.

A decent kisser.

Contained.

Good camouflage.

That fall, Priscilla left for Christian college in Oklahoma.

The night before she left, she made a mistake.

She asked me to take her place at church.

To sit with James.

To help keep him steady while she was gone.

She trusted me.

"I'd be happy to," I said.

The following Sunday, I adjusted the temperature.

My hand rested openly on his knee during service.

Fingers laced discreetly.

Attention redirected.

Territory shifts quietly when no one names it.

A few weeks later, there was a youth midnight bowling event.

James hesitated.

I didn't.

Before bowling, he took me to see The Muppet Movie.

I remember very little about Kermit.

After bowling, he parked outside my house.

I didn't get out.

I climbed into his lap.

The windows fogged.

There was a knock.

Not Daddy.

Bill.

In uniform.

Armed.

On duty.

He had seen James's car in officer housing and decided to investigate.

By the time we opened the door, Bill was furious.

Then he pivoted.

Tears.

Grandmother dying.

Immediate marriage.

Authority invoked like a badge.

"I could never marry you," I said.

And shut the door.

The next morning in choir, the lyrics said:

"Bring all of your needs to the altar…"

Bill took it literally.

He ran down the aisle mid-service and collapsed at the altar, sobbing.

The choir stopped.

The youth pastor stared at me.

The sanctuary stared harder.
After service, Bill asked Daddy for permission to marry me.
Proposal number five.
Apparently, I was still persuasive.
Just not in the direction anyone intended.

CHAPTER TWENTY

James had a real job.

Apprentice at a shipyard.

His own muscle car.

His own television.

He took me out to dinner every night.

In my world, that was practically a résumé.

I liked him more than anyone I'd ever met.

He even asked me on a real date.

He knocked on Daddy's door.

Daddy answered.

"Why are you here?" Daddy barked.

James swallowed.

"To take your daughter on a date, Sir."

Daddy grabbed him by the collar and hoisted him against the wall.

James's feet left the floor.

"Not with my daughter, you don't."

Quick as lightning, James said,

"Sorry, Sir. Wrong house!"

Daddy dropped him.

James bolted.

I came running down the hall screaming,

"Daddy! I like this one!"

By the time James peeled out of the driveway, I launched myself onto the hood of his Ford Maverick.

"Wait for me!"

"Not on your life!" he yelled.

I yanked open the door and dove inside.

"I love you! Don't ever leave me!"

For the first time, I wasn't performing.

But I also wasn't reformed.

I remained a social butterfly.

A psychology major took me for coffee after class.

Older.

Worked on the psych ward.

Clever.

He told me about Naugas — small, hairy forest creatures hunted for their hides to make toilet seat covers.

I believed him.

Repeated it confidently.

James dragged me back to the store to verify the story.

The clerk laughed.

"Naugahide is manmade. That boy invented the article."

James smirked.

I revised my sources.

From then on, we were officially courting.

And then there was Priscilla.

She had been "old-fashioned courting" James for years.

The church ladies had practically embroidered their future wedding date on a pillow.

Then I stepped in.

I wasn't finished.

I needed a maid of honor.

I couldn't think of anyone better than Priscilla.

During meet-and-greet one Sunday, in front of the senior matriarchs, I floated over and said sweetly:

"James and I are getting married mid-December — while you're home for break.

I would love for you to be my maid of honor, since you introduced us."

Silence.

The matriarchs leaned in.

Priscilla went pale.

I poured on honey.

"She's such a dear friend.

Such a loyal Christian."

The women pressed her.

She accepted.

I returned to my pew triumphant.

The church buzzed for weeks.

Would there be a scene?

Would I wear white?

Was I already pregnant?

Would it last?

Negative attention is still attention.

Daddy enforced his "No pre-marital hanky-panky" rule with an antique butter churn stick.

Every time James slid an arm around me —

Crack.

"Not in my house!"

James yelped.

Daddy laughed.

The wedding day arrived.

Small historic chapel.

Civil War moat.

One-lane bridge controlled by a stoplight.

Subtle symbolism was not our specialty.

Daddy officiated.

I dressed across the street in an old jail-cell office.

No stylist.

No theatrics.

Except the entire church was packed.

They lined the walls.

They didn't come for romance.

They came for spectacle.

James nearly didn't make it.
His best friend tried to talk him out of it.
Promised beaches.
Promised women.
Promised escape.
James stayed.
His car crossed the moat ten minutes before the ceremony.
I exhaled.
At 1:55 p.m., Daddy welcomed the crowd.
At 1:57 p.m., his face turned red.
He stumbled.
Then, abruptly:
"James, do you take Scarlett to be your lawfully wedded wife?"
James blinked.
"Yes… I think so, Sir."
"Scarlett, do you take James—"
"Yes, Daddy. You know I do."
"I now pronounce you husband and wife.
You may kiss the bride."
The chapel erupted.
Daddy pulled the butter churn stick from behind the pulpit and tapped James on the head.
We walked down the aisle.
2:00 p.m.
The administrative officer flung open the chapel doors.
Right on schedule.

CHAPTER TWENTY-ONE

More than a hundred people stood outside in bitter drizzle waiting to come into our wedding.

A little girl started crying.

I started yelling for Daddy.

He ran down the aisle and understood immediately.

When the first service had begun five minutes early — and the chapel was already full — the administrative specialist had posted the standard military chapel sign:

Service in Progress. Do Not Enter.

It was meant for tourists and early arrivals.

Instead, it trapped our wedding guests outside.

They had crossed the moat one car at a time, parked far away, walked through the cold — and now stood obediently waiting because the sign told them to.

Daddy's voice thundered through the sanctuary:

"Please give us a few minutes to empty the chapel, and we will do it all over again for you!"

Wedding number two.

The first group was ushered to the officers' club for the reception.

The second group flooded in.

At rehearsal we had planned:

• Candle lighting

• Kneeling at the altar

• The Lord's Prayer

• A soloist

• Words about families uniting

• Another solo before the vows

In reality, Daddy had skipped almost everything.

Straight to: "Do you?" and "I do."

Five minutes.

This time, he corrected himself.

We performed every ritual.

And then — just when I thought we were finished — Daddy launched into a thirty-minute sermon.

With an altar call.

People went forward for prayer while James and I sat beside our mothers, already married, waiting.

The first wedding lasted five minutes.

The second lasted an hour and a half.

After James kissed me, Daddy handed him the butter churn stick.

"Use this on your future daughter's boyfriends."

That was the inheritance.

By the time we reached the officers' club, the first group had eaten almost everything.

Except the cake.

We cut it.

Drank punch.

Twenty minutes later, it was over.

Priscilla kept her distance.

Glared through both ceremonies.

Posed for photographs with what can only be described as a stank face.

James's mother didn't look thrilled either.

Years later, as a grandmother, I keep those photos on my refrigerator.

I still giggle at them every morning.

James and I honeymooned at Disney World.

Back then, it was just Magic Kingdom.

We stayed off property.

Neither of our parents had explained sex to us.

They sent us with instructional books.

We read them on the flight.

During the day, we rode thrill rides.

At night, we followed directions.

One afternoon, stepping off a crowded elevator, we heard loud moaning and a bed slamming against the wall from the room across the hall.

Our room was directly opposite the elevator.

I turned crimson.

James looked petrified.

And that, my friends,

was the beginning of marriage.

CHAPTER TWENTY-TWO

I took a part-time job as the administrative assistant at a small Methodist church.

I told myself this was reform.

If I worked in a church office, surely goodness would seep into me through osmosis.

James would see the change.

Everyone would.

I stopped going out.

Attended church functions three nights a week.

We became youth leaders and earned a respectable place in leadership.

Respectable.

I also "learned to cook," which meant reheating frozen dinners and arranging them confidently on plates.

I had never washed dishes and saw no reason to begin.

Plates lived in the dishwasher until it was full.

At that point, I conducted inspections.

If a glass had developed mold, it went into the trash.

If a plate didn't come clean, it joined it.

Eventually we discovered paper plates.

A breakthrough in modern civilization.

One Sunday we invited James' parents and grandmother for lunch.

Wedding china.

Crystal goblets.

I decided it was time to debut my culinary skills.

Meatloaf.

Three pounds of hamburger.

One Durkee seasoning packet.

Ketchup.

Faith.

We prayed.

I brought it out with ceremony.

James' father sliced into it and a pink river escaped onto the china.

My mother-in-law calmly explained that three pounds of ground beef required lower heat and more time.

She split it lengthwise and returned half to the oven.

Thirty minutes later, I presented plates.

Father-in-law studied his serving.

"Would you like me to bring out the vegetables?"

Vegetables.

That had not occurred to me.

A few weeks later, a youth choir from out of state needed housing.

James and I volunteered to host two teenage boys.

We had recently purchased a yard-sale sleeper sofa — lumpy, optimistic, and historic.

My version of cleaning was efficient: move everything into the spare bedroom and shut the door.

In the car, the boys talked about how excited they were for a home-cooked Southern meal.

I beamed.

"Oh, you're getting fried chicken."

They were.

Banquet brand.

Overcooked.

Canned green beans.

Boxed mashed potatoes.

For dessert, I placed a Sara Lee cake on my grandmother's crystal stand.

I hadn't read the thawing instructions.

It was solid as concrete.

I sawed at it like lumber.

No one asked for seconds.

The next morning, wearing a bathrobe like Lucille Ball, I sashayed into the living room to make breakfast.

Both boys were asleep on the floor.

Apparently, the sleeper sofa had too many exposed springs and too much history.

"I'm making a home-cooked breakfast!" I announced.

They declined.

Needed to get to church early.

Hosting, I learned, is labor.

Recipes bored me.

Most dinners were eventually consumed at Putt-Putt Golf and Games or from the 7-11 deli case.

They had a miraculous new microwave that could heat a burrito in under a minute.

Innovation.

I wasn't incompetent.

I was uninterested.

That Thanksgiving, I invited relatives who lived three hours away — including the aunt who once produced a flawless holiday feast at her house.

She asked what she could bring.

"Nothing," I assured her.

"It's handled."

It was.

When they arrived, we chatted while the wedding china gleamed.

Aunt Melissa finally asked if she could help in the kitchen.

"Oh, it's ready."

I carried in a silver tray stacked with Wonder Bread, turkey cold cuts, cheese slices in cellophane, condiments, and a bowl of cranberry sauce.

Water in crystal goblets.

From the sink.

Silence settled over the table like snowfall.

Pecan ice cream was dessert.

I wasn't attempting pie.

They left shortly after.

That Thanksgiving has been retold at every family reunion since.

And I cannot argue with their version.

I wanted redemption.

Instead, I staged domestic theater.

Turns out salvation does not arrive through frozen chicken or wedding china.

But I committed to the role.

I always do.

CHAPTER TWENTY-THREE

Marriage did not cure me.

It adjusted the audience.

James expected a good Christian wife — breakfast early, lunch packed, dinner waiting.

Since I didn't cook, breakfast involved choices.

Cereal.

More cereal.

Sometimes a banana, sliced with ceremony as if that elevated the offering.

Lunch was where creativity thrived.

James never knew what would greet him at noon.

Peanut butter with banana and Miracle Whip.

Turkey with strawberry jam.

Peanut butter upgraded with ketchup.

He kept trusting me with this responsibility.

Eventually, he stopped.

When James came home from welding — clothes smelling like heat and metal — he carried whatever mood the day had welded into him.

He wanted something warm.

He got MTV.

If the evening soured, I'd go to bed irritated.

Sleep rarely cooperated, so I entertained myself.

I would lie still until his breathing evened out.

Then I'd tickle his ribs.

He'd jerk awake.

I'd retreat.

Silence.

When his breathing steadied again, I'd resume.

This could go on for a while.

In the morning, I'd massage his shoulders and ask softly,

"Did you sleep?"

"Not really."

"Maybe," I'd suggested, "your conscience was active."

Therapy followed.

The grumpiness lessened.

We rented a small house eventually.

A baby arrived.

The crib didn't fit in the spare bedroom because my cleaning strategy involved relocating chaos and closing doors.

James claimed the spare room.

I was assigned the refrigerator.

Shelf after shelf of expired experiments.

At the bottom, resting on a silver tray, sat a perfectly spherical bloom of rainbow mold.

Velvety purples.

Swirls of green.

It looked curated.

We lifted it out carefully for documentation.

I touched one corner.

The sphere collapsed into something swamp-like and aggressive.

Lettuce, it turns out, does not mature with dignity.

Then came the Vicodin episode.

The night my wisdom teeth were removed, we redeemed a long-saved hospital dinner coupon.

Steak.

Sides.

Complimentary wine.

I swallowed one pill before we left.

The cold air made my jaw throb, so I added another.

Wine arrived.

It disappeared.

While waiting for dessert, I rode the escalator upstairs to call my dentist and report that the medication seemed ineffective.

While on hold, I added a third.

By the time someone answered, the lighting felt interpretive.

The room began to sway when I hung up.

The escalator fascinated me.

Up.

Down.

Up again.

On one descent, I noticed the pastor's wife staring.

"I'm not drunk," I informed her.

"I'm very high."

She located James immediately.

Outside, in the parking lot, I reconsidered clothing.

Shoes came off.

Other items followed.

James intercepted me before the experiment reached its thesis stage.

I suggested privacy behind decorative bushes.

He informed me the highway ran directly behind them.

He secured me in the car and drove home, where his mother was babysitting.

They locked the bedroom door.

Vicodin privileges were revoked.

CHAPTER TWENTY-FOUR

James became a supervisor at work, and I took an admin job at a nearby military base — the same kind of base my daddy once worked on.

His grandmother babysat little Renee while we both worked long hours.

Between her and my mother-in-law, they handled breakfast, lunch, dinner, baths, diapers, and much of her wardrobe.

They kept her on weekends so we could sleep.

They took her to doctor's appointments and on long walks

In essence, they began raising my child.

My father-in-law didn't like what he saw.

One day, in a burst of anger, he told us we were unfit parents.

That was all it took.

Renee was removed from their care immediately and placed with a babysitter from church — someone who didn't come with commentary.

We kept attending church.

We led boys' and girls' scouting programs.

We rotated nursery duty and children's church.

That suited me just fine.

I had no interest in sitting through sermons when I could be shaping fourth, fifth, and sixth grade minds.

I preferred participation over passive listening.

One evening during a prayer circle, the girls shared their requests.

I shared one too.

In a moment of pregnancy fog at work, when a young woman called me a mean bitch, I hauled off and slapped her.

She fell to the floor.

I told the girls that while no one should hit another person, it is especially unwise to do so at your place of employment.

They gathered around me and prayed.

It hadn't occurred to me that the pastor's daughter was in that circle.

The next day I was summoned.

The pastor's wife read me the riot act for sharing such an "adult story" with impressionable girls.

I thought, *If you only knew the stories I chose not to share.*

The following week, James and I were demoted to teaching four-year-olds.

When Renee was eighteen months old, Bobby was born. That completed our family.

I quit working outside the home.

From the outside, we looked like a proper Christian family. Inside, I carried a quiet grudge toward my mother.

When Renee was born, she had said airfare was "too much of the Lord's money."

She didn't visit or send pictures.

I didn't call until my daughter was ten months old.

When Bobby was born, my mother came and stayed a month.

I slept.

I healed.

I tried not to unravel.

After she left, we moved thirty miles away from the in-laws.

I began babysitting neighborhood children the same age as mine.

I discovered I loved watching little minds ignite.

Crafts.

Letters.

Stories.

Church friends introduced me to homeschooling families.

I was handed math blocks, phonics charts, educational games.

Renee began reading early — not just sounding out words but comprehending full chapter books.

My father-in-law didn't believe it until she sat in his lap after Sunday lunch, read aloud from the *New York Times*, and explained the article back to him.

He looked stunned.

Maybe I wasn't unfit after all.

I taught every child in my care to read, write in full sentences, and add and subtract before kindergarten.

When school readiness tests showed Renee would place in first grade for math and second grade for English, I decided to homeschool permanently.

We joined a network of more than fifty homeschool families.

Field trips to the YMCA.

Skating rinks.

Co-op classes.

I started buying bulk grains from an Amish supplier and learned to make granola and bread from scratch.

Yes, I learned to cook.

I learned how to keep a house running.

The children thrived.

The floors stayed swept.

Homework finished before dinner.

Church friends nodded approval.

I wore the apron convincingly.

Flour dusted my hands.

Crayons littered the table.

Phonics in the morning. Fractions by afternoon.

I packed lunches that looked thoughtful.

Labeled math folders in careful script.

Smiled at co-op mothers who believed they understood the whole story.

They assumed I had retired.

They assumed softness had replaced ambition.
They mistook stillness for surrender.
They were wrong.
I wasn't reformed.
And I certainly wasn't subdued.
I had redirected.
George doesn't vanish. She adapts.
If I was going to be seen, it would be on my terms.
The apron was never an identity. It was a season.
Seasons change when I decide they do.
When I step forward again, I don't slip in quietly.
I arrive.

CHAPTER TWENTY-FIVE

I homeschooled my children until middle school, and then I enrolled them in private school.

By then, I had become something of an unexpected force.

I started attending Board of Education meetings as a homeschool mother, and I didn't sit quietly in the back.

Before long, the Governor appointed me Official Commissioner. I reviewed what students across our state would learn each year, grade by grade.

Yes.

Me.

The girl who once burned meatloaf and served cold cuts for Thanksgiving.

Now I was sitting at long polished tables with policymakers.

I was named lead on a committee for parent and business involvement in public schools.

I stood before crowds of hundreds — sometimes thousands — explaining new educational goals and gathering feedback.

I met with business leaders to determine what students actually needed to know to succeed in the workforce.

I listened.

I analyzed.

I reported.

And I held the Governor's ear.

One public meeting was held in a mega church in a neighboring city.

When I stepped out of the car with the Governor's entourage, I froze.

Priscilla.

James's former girlfriend.

She approached with perfect composure and introduced herself as the meeting coordinator.

She had spoken to me multiple times by phone and neither of us had realized who the other was.

She offered ice water for the podium.

I smiled sweetly.

"The Governor drinks bottled water," I said. "As do I."

When we were alone, the Governor asked what that was about.

"She might try to poison me," I replied calmly. "After what I did to her."

He blinked.

I did not elaborate.

Later that year, a former Governor's daughter invited James and me to her black-tie wedding.

We arrived underdressed and painfully aware of it.

I wore a short dress.

James wore a brown suit that had no business being in a ballroom of tuxedos.

The valet took the keys to our tired green station wagon.

James wanted to leave.

I wanted to feel like I belonged.

Inside, politicians circled me.

They wanted my opinion.

They wanted to know what I was hearing from parents.

What messaging would work.

What wouldn't.

James hovered nearby, uncomfortable and silent.

When the band shifted into modern music and younger guests flooded the dance floor, I overheard a cluster of opponents discussing language they had quietly inserted into an upcoming bill — wording designed to strip authority from the Governor's education reforms.

I didn't think.

I ran.

I climbed onto the stage, grabbed the Governor by his lapels, and pulled his ear down so I could whisper what I'd just overheard.

The music stopped.

The ballroom froze.

Four weapons were suddenly pointed at my chest.

I blinked slowly.

The Governor raised his hands.

"It's just Scarlett being Scarlett," he said. "She's no threat."

I stepped down.

James was gone.

He was outside by the station wagon, humiliated and furious.

The ride home was silent.

When the bills passed and the department was restructured, I resigned.

The stage dimmed.

For a minute.

Then I took a management role at a call center that handled everything from magazine subscriptions to pharmaceutical promotions, MTV vote-ins, and even a well-known psychic hotline.

I refused to take psychic calls on moral grounds and moved into Quality Assurance instead.

That is where my world exploded.

I supervised two hundred employees.

I listened to live and recorded calls for eight hours a day.

I trained employees to upsell.

To pronounce "valacyclovir hydrochloride" correctly.

To read scripts word-for-word.

If someone skipped more than three words, I could terminate them on the spot.

Turnover was high.

I didn't flinch.

Then came the people.

Two sweet older men ate lunch with me daily, gossiping like grandmothers.

One day I noticed matching handcrafted gold rings on their fingers.

They gently explained they were engaged.

They told me they felt safe around me because of the rainbow bumper sticker on my car.

I didn't know I had one.

I went outside and checked.

Sure enough — an Apple sticker with a rainbow logo.

The world was shifting.

Another supervisor wore flouncy dresses and a thinning wig.

I asked direct questions and learned about transgender identity.

When others gossiped, I defended her.

I even organized a collection to buy her a new wig.

This was the mid-1980s.

I was learning faster than I could process.

Then there was the dominatrix.

Covered in tattoos and piercings.

Always in black.

Chains.

Boots.

Scarlet lipstick.

Rumor had it she recruited teenage boys during training sessions for something called "the dungeon."

I was horrified.

And I was curious.

When I learned it was true — that two of my hires were sister wives in a BDSM household — Bondage, Discipline, Dominance, Submission, Sadism, Masochism — led by a man they called "Lord," I didn't fire them.

I leaned in.

I issued a written warning about workplace solicitation.

And then I asked questions.

Soon I found myself knocking on Lord's front door because official paperwork required his permission for his wife to sign government confidentiality forms.

The door opened.

A woman in lingerie greeted me.

I walked into a dim room lined with black carpet halfway up the walls.

Metal rings were bolted into the surfaces.

People were restrained.

A young man cried out as he was whipped.

Another knelt, painting a woman's toenails.

No one had told me this world existed.

I didn't recoil.

I observed.

Power dynamics fascinated me.

Who gives it.

Who takes it.

Who craves it.

I was ushered into a study expecting a handsome tyrant.

Instead, I met a man who looked like Jabba the Hutt.

And yet.

He commanded absolute loyalty.

My fierce, brash employee became soft-spoken in his presence.

I left that house with my paperwork signed and my mind racing.

⸙

My team also uncovered darker things.

A woman who kept a Bible on her desk was caught engaging in explicit phone sex with customers ordering kitchen appliances.

When I confronted her with security, she stood up — and both her chair and skirt were visibly wet.

I didn't look away.

I fired her.

Another employee arranged a drug deal on a live recorded line.

I coordinated with security and law enforcement.

A sting operation followed.

He never returned to work.

One frantic caller reported that an employee had used her personal information to stalk her across state lines.

Police were alerted.

The investigation was immediate.

By then, I was no longer naïve.

I was immersed in humanity.

Sex.

Control.

Fraud.

Deception.

Loneliness.

80

Power.

All of it played through a headset.

On Sundays I taught children.

At night I listened to adults unravel.

And somewhere inside, George was wide awake.

Not scandalized.

Not ashamed.

Not retreating.

Watching.

Learning.

Because the girl who once thought sex only happened at night had just walked through a dungeon and realized the world ran on far more complicated appetites than she had ever been taught.

I wasn't scared.

What I'd mistaken for a curtain call

had only ever been intermission.

CHAPTER TWENTY-SIX

I walked straight to his desk.

He hadn't shown up for work that night.

I called security and the officer who had recently been posted in our building.

Representatives weren't allowed to have paper or writing utensils at their desks — immediate termination if they did.

Too much personal information passed through those headsets.

The police opened his drawer.

Inside was a stack of Post-it notes.

Names.

Addresses.

Phone numbers.

Personal details.

Notes about single women.

He wasn't just sloppy.

He was hunting.

After running his records, the police came back to me with a simple directive:

Terminate him immediately.

I signed the paperwork without hesitation.

By then I had begun asking myself a different question:

Why did our call center seem to attract so many damaged souls?

My director didn't waste time wondering.

He contacted city police and made our building an official break stop for every squad car in the district.

Officers rotated through constantly.
Coffee in hand.
Guns visible.
It made management feel better.
Not safe.
Just better.

One afternoon, I accompanied my son to traffic court so he could obtain his driver's license.

Before his case was called, a string of juvenile offenders shuffled in — drugs, robbery, reckless driving.

The judge gave each of them a choice.

Jail time.

Or community service and mandatory employment.

Then he asked a question that made my stomach tighten.

"Can you read and write?"

If they said yes, he nodded and said,

"Good. Get a job at the call center. They'll hire anyone."

The courtroom laughed.

I did not.

Apparently, intermission was over.

Around that time, I became close friends with another manager in the building — Amy.

We went to lunch together.

We shopped together.

James treated us to dinners at restaurants that pretended to be exotic.

Our families blended easily.

Our teenage kids adored her.

Survivor had just premiered, so every Thursday night we hosted watch parties with two oversized televisions in the living room and bowls of snacks on every surface.

Amy became family.

She was from Long Island.

Her apartment looked like it belonged in Better Homes and Gardens.

Everything coordinated.

Pillows matched curtains.

Curtains matched the throw blanket.

Her outfits looked like they were lifted straight from a catalog.

My house?

Let's just say it had personality.

James and I were relaxed.

Slightly chaotic.

Comfortable in imperfection.

Amy was polished.

Structured.

Contained.

We were opposites.

Which, as I was beginning to learn, is exactly what draws certain people together.

And I have always been fascinated by contrast.

CHAPTER TWENTY-SEVEN

James and I took the kids to Disney World, SeaWorld, and Universal Studios several times a year.

Annual passes were our version of stocking stuffers.

If there was a roller coaster within driving distance, we were on it.

When Universal sent a "bring a guest free" invitation, I invited Amy.

I wanted to impress her.

Show her our world.

Show her how we had fun.

We bought tickets to the Pirates dinner show in Orlando — the one with the full-size pirate ship replica in the middle of a cavernous arena.

We were seated with the Red Group.

No utensils were handed out.

Amy looked confused.

"You eat with your hands," I whispered, delighted.

The pirate wenches dropped heavy platters of meat and vegetables in front of us and filled our goblets with mead.

I tasted mine.

Didn't love it.

So, I chugged it.

It was immediately refilled.

I chugged again.

Refilled.

Again.

Apparently, the system rewarded enthusiasm.

Each section was assigned a pirate to root for in the battle for gold and the captured maiden.

Our red-sashed pirate strutted onto the stage, and I committed fully.

Amy sipped her mead like a debutante.

James nursed his.

I roared like a dockworker.

By the end of the show, I was slurring and unsteady, passionately invested in the Red Pirate's future.

He lost.

This did not sit well with me.

After the show, the pirates lined up for photos.

James and Amy half-carried me through the line.

When I reached my red-sashed disappointment, I wrapped my arms around his neck and shouted in his face,

"You SUCK! You made us lose!" I slurred.

"You didn't win the gold or the girl! You need pirate school!"

The poor man thrashed like he was being attacked by a barnacle.

Amy's face went pale.

James looked like he wanted to disappear into the plank.

They carried me to the car, up the hotel elevator, and deposited me on the bed — fully dressed, shoes and all.

The next morning was Universal Studios.

Amy had confessed the night before that she was afraid of heights.

Confessed.

To me.

That was her mistake.

An idea formed instantly.

I shared it with James.

He hesitated.

Then he grinned.

We walked Amy into what looked like an innocent one-story building.

No towering tracks outside.

No obvious danger.

Inside was a long, dim corridor.

We kept her distracted, talking over each other, steering her forward.

We passed through another dark hallway and suddenly found ourselves at the front of a line in total darkness.

Screams echoed somewhere beyond the walls.

Amy stiffened.

The doors opened.

Sixteen seats arranged in a circle around a pole.

"Wait. What. What is this?" she stammered.

Before she could process the answer, a cast member buckled her in between James and me.

She leaned forward to ask again.

James shoved her gently but firmly into her seat.

The alarm sounded.

And the entire ring of seats shot straight into the sky.

Weightless.

Amy shrieked.

We dropped halfway down.

Shot back up.

Dropped again.

Her mouth opened but no words came out.

By the time we hit the ground for the final time, all three of us had rubber legs.

Amy did not laugh.

She told us off in language that would've made a pirate proud.

I apologized.

Convincingly.

Inside, I was howling.

James promised her no more tall rides.

We strolled through the park afterward, sticking to tame attractions.

Every time we passed the tower, Amy glared at it like it had personally assaulted her.

James and I exchanged silent glances.

We knew.

The next morning, boarding our Southwest flight home, Amy turned to us and said calmly,

"I think I need a break from you two."

A break?

From fun?

I blinked.

"We had a great time," I insisted. "You should come next trip."

She did not respond.

And that was when it finally dawned on me.

Not everyone experiences chaos as joy.

Some people experience it as trauma.

Apparently, intermission really was over.

And I was still playing to a crowd that wasn't laughing anymore.

CHAPTER TWENTY-EIGHT

A few months later, Amy came back.

Like nothing had happened.

We were best friends again — weekly dinners with James and the teenagers, long lunches, laughter restored.

Whatever fracture had formed at Universal seemed to seal itself over.

Until the tornado.

One afternoon at work, my phone rang.

Amy was sobbing.

A tornado had tracked along the interstate for sixty miles and dropped straight over the military installation near her apartment complex.

It had skimmed low across her building.

Part of the roof was gone.

A vehicle had been thrown against her glass doors.

She had to evacuate.

But she couldn't get to her car.

I didn't hesitate.

I sped home, grabbed James — because James was steady when I wasn't — and we drove straight to her.

We collected Amy and her cat and installed them in a hotel for the night.

The next afternoon, emergency services allowed residents twenty minutes inside their units if the structure was deemed stable.

James, practical as ever, told Amy to empty her laundry hamper into a trash bag.

At least she'd have a week's worth of work clothes.

She grabbed shoes, a few more outfits, and we hustled out before our twenty minutes were up.

That night, James insisted she move in with us until the apartment was rebuilt.

Amy fit into our life like she'd always been there.

She walked James' dog.

She took the kids on outings.

She grocery shopped with me.

She cooked meals that didn't involve seasoning packets or boxed potatoes.

Upscale.

Balanced.

Proper.

I watched and learned.

Black mold stretched her displacement into four months.

Four months of shared dinners and laughter and late-night conversations.

When her apartment was finally restored and she moved back out, I felt like I'd lost a sister.

At work, I was in charge of contest prizes — the samples companies sent for employee incentives.

Exercise equipment.

Kitchen gadgets.

Beauty kits.

Even press-on nails.

Inventory started disappearing.

And I do not like missing pieces.

I'd heard rumors about our director being generous with certain subordinates.

Money splashing.

Favors exchanged.

I started watching.

Quietly.

Parking lots.

Hand-offs.

Patterns.

I loathe people who abuse power.

And I loathe people who build pedestals and expect applause.

So, I did what any good detective would.

I followed the trail.

One Saturday morning, I pulled up to his house.

And there it was.

A yard sale.

Not just any yard sale — a glittering display of call center prize inventory.

Exercise machines.

Kitchen appliances.

Weight loss tapes.

Hair tools.

Press-on nail sets.

My inventory.

I took photos.

Clear ones.

Then I marched straight past Human Resources and into the office of the Vice President of Marketing — the man who oversaw our entire operation.

I laid everything on his desk.

And then I handed him my resignation.

Effective immediately.

He blinked.

Then asked me to stay two weeks.

Bonus pay.

No retaliation.

He promised.

Monday morning, I walked into what was supposed to be our regular director meeting.

His secretary stopped me at the door, pressed a finger to her lips, and quietly unlocked the office.

The Vice President was sitting in the director's chair.

Two chairs were positioned in front of the desk — spaced far apart.

We waited.

My director was habitually late.

Everyone knew it.

When he finally walked in and saw the Vice President in his seat, the color drained from his face.

The Vice President outlined the evidence.

Calmly.

Precisely.

Then he told him that if there was any retaliation toward me, charges would follow.

The director resigned on the spot.

I walked out shaking.

Not because I was afraid.

Because I had just toppled someone.

And part of me — the George part — had enjoyed it.

I began looking for another job that afternoon.

The apron was off again.

And the stage lights were warming.

CHAPTER TWENTY-NINE

I landed a position with Amy at a different kind of call center — one that took incoming orders for men's and women's clothing.

No psychic hotlines.

No pharmaceutical pronunciations.

Just fashion and fast talk.

I caught on quickly.

Upsells?

Child's play.

Soon my team held the number one spot in sales and call statistics.

After that I rotated through Quality Assurance.

Then Customer Service.

Then email orders started trending, so I built an email and chat team from scratch.

When the company decided to move customer service overseas, they sent me to Nova Scotia in January to train the new team.

January.

In Canada.

There were feet of snow on the ground.

The office sat on an isthmus in the Atlantic Ocean, though no one bothered to explain that part to me at first.

I arrived bundled in three layers, hats, gloves, scarves — looking like a walking laundry basket.

The first morning, I stepped out of my rental car and the wind hit me so hard it lifted my boots off the ground and slid me toward the building like I was auditioning for Olympic ice skating.

Arms out.

Eyes wide.

I slid through the front door without breaking stride.

The Canadian employees stood and applauded.

I peeled off hats, gloves, sweaters, one layer at a time while they giggled at the American snow woman who had just wind-surfed her way into work.

I asked where the refrigerator was to put my lunch.

The director led me out the back door.

"To the fridge."

It was a snow drift.

When in Canada.

I told him the area must be beautiful in summer with all the green space and soccer fields nearby.

He looked at me strangely.

He did not answer.

Later that evening, another American and I decided to find dinner.

There was exactly one restaurant in town.

I had directions.

It was snowing heavily, but I drove slowly and responsibly.

We turned onto a one-way street.

There were houses at first.

Then suddenly there weren't.

The road narrowed.

Fog rolled in.

Snow thickened.

My passenger screamed.

Ahead of us was a "Do Not Enter" sign with metal boards blocking the way.

If you remember, dear reader, I am not good at driving in reverse.

I am catastrophically bad at driving in reverse.

The road was too narrow for us to switch seats.

So I did what any rational adult would.

I backed up.

Five miles per hour.

On ice.

For nearly an hour.

Eventually we saw flashing red and blue lights.

Police vehicles.

Neighbors had called them.

Apparently, I had been driving down a fishing pier over the Atlantic Ocean.

Those "soccer fields" I'd admired earlier?

Frozen ocean waves.

The Canadians had assumed we were attempting suicide.

I was relieved to return home alive a few days later.

I thought that would be the peak of my international embarrassment.

It wasn't.

Back at the office, I was called into a hush-hush meeting with a Chinese contingent that owned a call center in the Philippines.

The company was closing domestically.

All calls were moving overseas.

I had been selected to lead the training team in Manila.

Of course I had.

Upon arrival, the three Americans and two Canadians assigned to the project gathered in a shared hotel suite.

We introduced ourselves:

One gay man.

One straight man.

One bisexual woman.

One straight woman.

And me — vibrating with excitement.

We looked at each other and wondered if hidden cameras were filming us for a reality show.

We checked the lamps and

The smoke detectors.

The mirrors.

No cameras.

Just destiny.

The local call center manager and his Filipina girlfriend arranged outings so we could "experience the culture."

One excursion took us to a volcano in Tagaytay.

We were to cross a lake first in an outrigger canoe.

I asked to use the restroom.

The boat captain led me to a three-sided plastic shed and pointed to a bucket.

Bless my grandmother for teaching me to keep tissues in my purse.

Men stood nearby.

I learned quickly how to squat with dignity under observation.

The captain handed me a life jacket that would have snugly fit a six-year-old.

I asked for another.

I wore them on my arms like inflatable floaties.

The water was calm.

The scenery was lush.

It felt magical.

We rode donkeys up the mountain.

The donkey beneath my American weight protested loudly and stopped often to reconsider his life choices.

At the top, tourists walked a narrow path around the volcano's rim.

The trail was barely two feet wide and bowed in the center from centuries of foot traffic.

Everyone else was peering into molten lava.

I noticed a chained-off area ahead with skull-and-crossbones warning signs.

Most people avoid skulls.

I recruit Scandinavians.

I convinced two tall, gorgeous men to follow me beyond the chain so we could "see if the steam made the rocks hot."

They did.

The rocks were hot.

And sticky.

Then a blast of steam shot out.

We ran.

I tripped.

And I rolled.

Head, butt, knees.

Head, butt, knees.

Like a bowling ball in a human alley.

The bowed pathway saved me from tumbling into lava or off the mountain entirely, but I was gaining speed.

Thirty feet down, the massive call center manager lunged forward and caught me mid-roll.

My knees were bleeding.

My scalp was split.

My clothes were torn.

We left immediately.

Those poor donkeys deserved hazard pay on the descent.

To this day, I still have a piece of lava embedded in the top of my head.

No metaphor. Actual lava.

CHAPTER THIRTY

I trained the Quality Assurance team and the managers while the others rotated class after class of fresh recruits through the training rooms.

The first thing I noticed in that country was that nothing was wasted.

Not paper.

Not space.

Not people.

The printer paper they handed me had résumés on the back.

I flipped one over and nearly dropped it.

Age.

Marital status.

Pregnancy status.

Religion.

Parents' employment.

Household income.

As casually listed as eye color.

Then I saw the medical testing files.

Mandatory pregnancy tests.

STD panels.

Blood pressure.

Heart health.

Drug screens.

Mental health screenings.

And every single employee?

Young women.

Twenty-one to twenty-four.

Fresh out of college.

Beautiful.

Thin.
I asked the owner about it.
He didn't flinch.
He showed me the newspaper ads.
Some companies hired only men.
Some hired only men over five foot six.
Banks hired "presentable young women from good families."
It was just business.
Once I understood the game, I told him,
"You need men."
He raised an eyebrow.
I explained that American women often responded better to a male sales voice.
He agreed to a trial class.
The following Monday, I walked into the classroom and stopped cold.
Twenty men.
In dresses.
Heels.
Bras.
Perfect eyeliner.
Confidence for days.
The owner shrugged.
"Best I could do. They know fashion."
I sat down and listened.
It was my first time leading a training room full of cross-dressers and drag performers.
They were sharp.
Quick.
Funny.
And every one of them spoke in a high, breathy register.
I went to HR.

"Would it be inappropriate," I asked sweetly, "to coach them toward a deeper tone for American callers?"

For one week, I lined them up in two rows.

"Again."

"Lower."

"Ground it."

"Smile with your eyes, not your throat."

We tested it.

Two weeks high voice.

Two weeks lower voice.

Upsells doubled during the lower-voice phase.

They were hired permanently.

Turns out femininity is an art form — and so is strategy.

Culture shock kept unfolding.

Trainees were allowed to read *Playgirl* and *Maxim* in class.

Every month, the women were pregnancy tested during drug screens.

The results were posted publicly on the bathroom door next to their full names.

Pregnant?

Fired.

Positive STD?

Fired.

Drugs?

Fired.

Contraceptives were nearly impossible to find legally.

Many feminine hygiene products weren't stocked openly either.

The girls told me quietly that if they couldn't control pregnancy, they couldn't keep their jobs.

They lived in dormitories on site.

They had no privacy, no leverage.

So I started making weekly supply runs to American and Australian grocery stores.

Condoms.

Contraceptives.

Hygiene products.

I became the quiet courier of autonomy.

Nobody announced it.

Nobody thanked me loudly.

But the girls knew.

When our "two-month assignment" quietly stretched longer, I asked my American team what they needed.

One woman said, "A vibrator."

I had never seen one outside of a joke.

One man wanted a Playgirl.

Another wanted Playboy.

Everyone needed condoms.

I didn't know where to get any of it.

The boy-girls did.

They took me to a former presidential mansion turned drag nightclub.

Upstairs was something else entirely.

Entrance fee?

Four U.S. dollars.

I stood on a grand staircase watching bodies move like freedom had finally been uncaged.

After an hour I said,

"Alright. I need to shop."

A tall man took my hand with ceremony.

"Do not look left or right.

Follow only me."
Upstairs, I saw small cubicles with beds.
Heard people moaning.
A naked boy ran past me.
I was not scandalized.
I was processing.
Curiosity and caution were arm wrestling inside my chest.
We climbed again.
A tiled palace room.
Fountains.
Men being bathed.
Lush plants crawling up mosaic walls.
I had grown up in a Baptist church.
And here I was.
Following a man past a leather door handle shaped like something I had never seen mounted on a knob before.
Another first.
Inside, velvet.
Sandalwood.
Jewel tones.
An enormous man greeted me like royalty.
I handed him my list.
No browsing.
No wandering.
Playgirl.
Playboy.
Condoms.
Lubricant.
A vibrator.
He returned with magazines fifteen years old — relics from a closed naval base.
Ten dollars each.
Then the toys.

Leather.
Ball gags.
Chains.
He demonstrated four vibrators.
I did not pretend expertise.
"You choose," I said.
He chose the most expensive.
Five boxes of condoms.
Twenty tubes of lubricant.
Under five hundred dollars.
He packed it all and ushered me down a metal fire escape.
Only then did I realize the performance.
The stairs.
The chanting.
The door.
The palace.
It was theater.
And I had bought a ticket.

A few days before my birthday, the owner summoned me.
Pearls.
Custom suits.
A mountain retreat.
I declined.
Instead, I requested:
A vacation day for every agent.
A staff-wide after-hours celebration.
And the upper management men — wives included — to attend
a party in our suite.
He agreed.

For months, my team had plastered *Playboy* and *Playgirl* spreads over the walls.

They made me laugh.

For the party, I covered them with tourist maps.

I bought twenty-five bottles of expensive liquor because I had no idea how much was "enough."

Apparently six would've done.

The wives arrived in elaborate gowns inspired by Imelda Marcos — dramatic sleeves, heavy tapestry, trailing trains.

One asked for wine.

I handed her a juice glass with a tiny bottle.

Paper cups were all we had.

After dinner, I took the men into another room.

One glass.

Five executives.

Wild Turkey Rare Breed.

No chasers.

They gagged.

I took two shots straight and smiled.

Eventually, they were relaxed enough to forget titles.

When I returned to the wives, one had fished an old *Playboy* out of the couch cushions.

They were huddled together, whispering.

Comparing anatomy.

Asking whether American men were "all like that."

I assessed the temperature in the room.

Time to shut this down before international relations required explanation.

The next morning, hungover executives asked what happened.

I shrugged.

I never lie.

I just don't always explain.

CHAPTER THIRTY-ONE

The call center manager was a Brit, and once a week at the end of shift, just as the sun began threatening the horizon, he'd take me for a "proper British breakfast" in the red-light district.

Yes.

That's a sentence I just wrote.

We'd sit outside at an open-air nightclub while waitresses in heels and glitter drifted in and out.

The driver — a silver-haired man in his late sixties — stood nearby like a sentry.

He carried a weapon large enough to discourage curiosity and made sure strangers didn't wander too close.

We always ate outside.

Inside was "no place for a lady."

Which, of course, meant I was curious.

One morning around five, I decided I was done pretending.

"I need the restroom," I said sweetly, and slipped inside.

There were only a few patrons left, so when I held up U.S. dollars, the dancers swarmed like I'd rung a bell.

They pulled me onstage.

Taught me how to grip the pole with my thighs.

How to arch.

How to laugh with my shoulders.

We danced for thirty solid minutes.

When I stepped back outside, flushed and triumphant, I noticed something.

A small crowd had gathered.

They weren't looking at me.

They were looking up.

Monitors hung from the ceiling, broadcasting the interior feed.

There I was.

On multiple screens.

Gyrating.

The British manager stood with his arms folded, trying not to smirk.

I was embarrassed.

And also?

Pleased.

Apparently, I'd picked up a new skill set.

Tee hee.

Another night, a group of my female agents asked if I'd take them to a European bar.

They couldn't enter without a foreigner.

"Well," I said, "I do have a passport."

We dressed up and went to the more polished part of town.

Chandeliers.

Marble floors.

Techno pulsing like a heartbeat.

I paid my entrance fee.

The girls were free.

Men immediately began asking them to dance.

As long as my girls were smiling, I was content to sit back and sip my drink.

Then a man sat beside me and handed me cash.

I blinked.

Another did the same.

That's when I noticed the screens behind the bar were playing porn.

And the back wall had doors.

Private rooms.

My girls disappeared inside with men and reappeared glowing and giggling.

I did the math.

Apparently, I had once again been mistaken for a madame.

I laughed.

If I'd known commission was involved, I might've negotiated.

About a month before we were scheduled to go home, corporate announced an inspection visit.

We worked like soldiers preparing for war.

Spreadsheets perfect.

Metrics polished.

Training manuals aligned.

On the day of arrival, I went to the airport to greet the executive.

It was HR.

Someone I knew.

Instead of heading to the car, he pulled me into a small conference room.

He opened his briefcase like he was about to present an award.

"The U.S. call center is closing," he said calmly.

"You're being laid off upon arrival home."

He slid paperwork across the table.

Then he stood.

Boarded the next flight.

Left me there to break the news to my team.

I went back to the hotel and stared at the ceiling.

Then I wrote an email.

Precise.

Professional.

Unshakeable.

I explained that their layoff date made no logistical sense — we would land after HR closed.

No reimbursement.

No benefits review.

No job search window.

If they were going to cut us loose, they were going to do it cleanly.

I cried that morning.

But I did not beg.

That night at work, around midnight, the building began to move.

At first, it felt like dizziness.

Then alarms screamed.

A 6.8 earthquake.

We were on the twenty-second floor.

The tower rocked like it had been shoved by an angry god.

I stood — and my body flew.

From my office window.

Through the open doorway.

Into the office across the hall.

Back and forth.

Like a human pendulum.

The Brit braced himself in my doorway and grabbed me mid-flight.

The moment I stopped moving, I grabbed the phone.

"James," I yelled, "we're in an earthquake. I think I'm going to die. If I do, remember I love you."

Then the line cut.

The building began to spin.

When it slowed, I shoved my feet into tennis shoes and walked down twenty-two flights of stairs.

In the courtyard, I collapsed beside an old war tank turned sculpture.

I shook.

I sobbed.

A foreigner knelt beside me and handed me a cherry cigarette.

He thought I was crying about the earthquake.

I was crying about the earthquake… and losing my job… and five years of loyalty evaporating in a conference room.

Between aftershocks, I told him.

He listened.

He introduced himself.

He lived less than an hour from me back home.

He'd heard of "A'te Scarlett."

The agents spoke well of me.

Especially the girls.

A few cherry cigarettes and several tremors later, he said casually:

"That was an informal interview. I'm calling my director tomorrow."

I stared at him.

Of course you are.

Because apparently, even seismic activity works in my favor.

When I finally returned home, James looked like he'd aged a decade.

When I'd called him during the quake, he'd been leading a national disaster recovery meeting.

He took my call mid-sentence.

Turned white.

Sat down.

The room had nearly called a medic.

He told them what I'd said.

The room fell silent.

Nothing like a real disaster to sharpen a disaster preparedness briefing.

He couldn't reach me for two days.

Did it occur to me to call and reassure him sooner?

It did not.

I was busy surviving.

We both needed a break.

Fortunately, I'd been hired by the American man from the courtyard.

Two weeks off before the new job.

Time to breathe.

Or so we thought.

ACT III: RECALIBRATION

CONFESSION OF RECALIBRATION

I thought I was climbing.

I didn't realize I was accelerating.

There's a difference.

One feels like growth.

The other feels like flight.

I kept saying yes to bigger rooms, louder music, higher bridges, stronger currents. Somewhere along the way I mistook motion for momentum.

And when the building shook—when the ground moved without asking me—I understood something I had refused to learn.

You don't control intensity.

You borrow it.

And borrowed power always comes due.

The earthquake didn't scare me as much as it should have.

I survived.

Again.

That was the problem.

Because surviving starts to feel like permission.

Until your body makes a decision your mouth never would.

The truth?

I wasn't fearless.

I was untethered.

And recalibration doesn't arrive gently.

It interrupts.

It stops the car.

It silences the mouth.

It takes the numbers away.

It forces you to ask:

If I cannot outrun it...

Who am I without the edge?

— Scarlett

CHAPTER THIRTY-TWO

We chose a cruise.

Our first.

Being the type-A planner that I am, I treated it like a military operation. Excursions booked. Dinner reservations locked in. Schedules color-coded in my head.

The day before sailing, we were lounging by the pool at our Miami hotel when our twenty-one-year-old daughter called.

She'd gotten off work early.

"Y'all wanna go to dinner?"

I smiled into the phone. "Baby, we can't. We're in Miami. We sail tomorrow."

There was a pause.

Then a whimper.

"I can't believe you're going on a cruise without me!"

I reminded her gently that months earlier, when we'd mentioned the idea, she'd laughed and declared, "Cruises are for OLD people."

So we didn't invite her.

Her silence told me she regretted that statement.

Which is when the prank was born.

I decided we would tell her it was actually a Spring Break cruise — packed with cute, single, young men everywhere.

And to prove it?

I would collect photographic evidence.

Once onboard, I began recruiting.

"Excuse me, would you and your friends mind posing for a quick picture? It's for my daughter."

Word spread across the ship.

Young fathers handed babies to their wives and jumped into photos.

Twenty-somethings with beers posed by the pool.

Groups gathered in the casino, on the deck, in the bars.

By midweek I had an entire catalog of handsome men grinning into my camera.

Our daughter was flummoxed.

Exactly as intended.

The first two days were sublime.

Then the excursion tickets arrived.

James picked them up from the bed and read aloud.

"Swim with the Sharks."

He stared at me.

"What are you trying to do, Woman? Get us killed?"

In my sweetest voice, I explained, **"Oh no, dear. I only have a boat ticket. You're the only one getting in."

His eyes widened.

"So you're just trying to kill me?"

"The brochure says they're nurse sharks," I cooed. "They won't bite you!"

"Is there a sign in the ocean?" he demanded. **"Nurse sharks only? No great whites allowed past this point? Can they read?"

Perhaps I had miscalculated.

While he sputtered, I debated whether to mention his other excursion.

Zip-lining through the jungle.

Over waterfalls.

I decided to hold that one in reserve.

The next morning, we visited the excursion desk.

115

We compromised on snorkeling.

But only after I swore — repeatedly — to stay right by his side in the water.

He's near-sighted and did not want to surface and discover he'd joined the wrong tour group.

That detail will matter later.

The water was clear and bright.

We were assigned to follow a buoy with a Mexican flag and the number seven.

James grew braver with each dive, following the guides deeper to see the fish below.

I, on the other hand, could not hold my breath long enough to be impressive.

So I floated.

Watched.

Drifted.

The guides moved to another area, chumming the water. Fish gathered in glittering schools.

I followed.

Mesmerized.

Then I followed them back to the boat.

Where tequila was introduced.

The crew poured generously.

After a few shots, it tasted… festive.

I did belly shots.

Danced on deck.

Floated in a sarong like I'd been born for maritime revelry.

Occasionally the captain called roll.

"Scarlett?"

"Heeeeere!"

"James?"
"Heeeeere!"
I answered for both of us.
After several roll calls, the captain announced,
"We are missing one person."
I continued dancing.
Apparently, another tour boat radioed in.
They had acquired a passenger.
A near-sighted man who, upon surfacing from his final dive, couldn't read the buoy numbers and followed the wrong group.
He had chosen poorly.
They dropped James into the water so he could swim back to his rightful boat.
When he climbed aboard, the captain reamed him out for delaying their return.
"Who was answering 'here' during roll call?" the captain demanded.
James pointed.
"See the red-headed drunk woman dancing on the table? I'm with her."
The captain looked at me.
Shrugged.
"Vaya con Dios."
Go with God.
That should've been my warning.
Instead, I kept dancing.
When we returned to the ship, James and two crew members carried me to our cabin.
I was placed on the bed like contraband.
The doghouse was entered shortly thereafter.
The remainder of the cruise was… quieter.
Apparently nurse sharks weren't the real threat.
Tequila was.

CHAPTER THIRTY-THREE

Now that my children were older, my preacher parents visited regularly.

The drive took two days, which meant I always had warning.

The Sunday before their arrival, I would sprint to the neighborhood Baptist church right after services ended. I'd scoop up four leftover bulletins from the empty pews like contraband and rush home for what I called an Emergency Holiness Summit.

We read the sermon scripture.

I retold the Bible story.

We strategically placed Bibles throughout the house with bulletins sticking out conspicuously.

Then came the Purge.

Posters down.

Secular books hidden.

Anything remotely questionable vanished.

James cleared the liquor cabinet.

I replaced coffee table books with wholesome Christian devotionals.

Most of the time, it worked.

Except the time Grandma discovered a scantily clad Britney Spears poster taped behind my grandson's bedroom door.

That sermon lasted three hours.

At my new job, I decided to become technical.

Which is hysterical, because I am not technical.

I took classes.

Took notes.

Memorized troubleshooting trees.

Earned top scores on every test.

Then we went live.

And I floundered like a dying catfish.

I raised my hand.

Every.

Single.

Call.

After two hours, I was removed from the phones and told to go "review the HR handbook."

Instead, I double-jacked my headset into my team's calls and studied them like an anthropologist.

Which screens they used.

What shortcuts they took.

How they calmed angry customers.

I would learn.

My manager did not want me there.

He admitted he had objected to hiring a supervisor from outside who lacked technical knowledge.

That was all I needed to hear.

I read every manual.

Every policy.

Every HR guideline.

Then I went straight to the director who hired me.

"Why me?" I asked.

He smiled.

"I need a change agent."

Well then.

Let's change things.

I noticed supervisors were partially shutting down phone lines before lunch.

And before the end of the day.

To go home on time.

Meanwhile customers were getting busy signals.

I reported it.

At the next supervisors' meeting, it was addressed.

I became persona non grata.

I did not mind.

Ostracism has never frightened me.

They began watching me.

Gossiping.

Waiting for mistakes.

I was handed underperformers.

New hires.

Weak technical support.

It felt like a setup.

So I built.

When a corporate cost-cutting visitor arrived, I told him exactly what was happening.

We rearranged support.

We secretly began mentoring a new team lead.

We trained in shadows.

I promised my team two sheet cakes when we became number one.

One to celebrate.

One to rub noses in.

We hit number one.

Both cakes were delivered.

I have never enjoyed cake more.

Tanisha.
My new team lead.
Also a rebellious preacher's daughter.
Also competitive.
Also dangerous in the best way.
For weeks we communicated only by Post-It notes.
Eventually we became trench soldiers.
We trained after hours.
On weekends.
In secret.
People began whispering.
Accusing.
Speculating.
Someone sang in the hallway:
"Scarlett and Tanisha sitting in a tree..."
We laughed.
Then an agent told Tanisha's preacher-wife mother that we were
having an affair.
Cruelty is always louder than truth.
But our team?
They loved us.
That was enough.

The Great Chili Cook-Off.
We named ours "The 12 Days of Christmas."
Each agent added candy.
Chocolate bars.
Peppermints.

Lemon drops.

Black licorice.

Hogwarts jelly beans.

It was horrifying.

It won first place.

When people crowded for the recipe, we posted photos of every candy addition.

By 3 p.m., supervisors were sprinting to bathrooms.

Revenge tastes like sugar and regret.

Then jail called.

An agent had been sentenced for reckless driving.

He couldn't reach his wife.

So at 9:30 p.m., Tanisha and I drove through a dark subdivision looking for a Volkswagen and twin car seats.

We found the house.

I knocked.

His wife screamed,

"Are you sleeping with him?"

I calmly explained I was his supervisor.

For two weeks I became their jailhouse operator.

"Tell her I love her."

"She says she hates you."

"She loves you."

When he returned to work, the team wore prison orange.

That's bonding.

Then Tanisha and I staged a fake make-out session under a mega church security camera.

Just to see what would happen.
Security chased us.
We went to a bar.
I call that cardio.

My team pranked me back once.
They held my keyboard hostage.
Sent ransom notes by paper airplane.
Made me tap dance in the breakroom.
I complied.
Team building works both ways.

I had, by this time, acquired what some might call… accessories.
My glass cubicle wall displayed Japanese bondage anime in dark jewel
tones—two panels depicting a princely man reclining on a chaise
lounge while a woman stood over him holding a cat-o'-nine-tails.
My bottom drawer held fuzzy handcuffs, rubber leg irons,
chains, ball gags.
Yes.
I supervised metrics by day and collected curiosities by night.
One day Japanese corporate visitors noticed the artwork.
The CEO smiled knowingly.
I opened the drawer.
They gasped.
I bowed.
We went out for Wild Turkey shots.
Then midnight Walmart.
They taught me how to measure bra size by holding panties
around my neck.

My manager nearly fainted when he found me at breakfast with them the next morning.

The executives invited me to their corporate lunch.

In my Walmart outfit.

Sometimes you win by being exactly who you are.

James bought me a silver Honda SUV.

I traded it for a gunmetal Civic without telling him.

Licked the car to claim it.

Signed the paperwork.

He screamed.

I giggled.

Naturally.

Then I decided to test the Civic in a tunnel.

105 mph.

I had calculated the state troopers' blind spots.

I had not calculated that the slow-moving truck was following a trooper.

License suspended for a year.

No driving privileges.

The judge bellowed.

James bellowed louder.

For weeks he drove me like a chauffeur.

Then I moved into three different houses during the week and rotated wardrobes by color.

Eventually I stayed with a childless couple.

We went to gay nightclubs.

I told people we were family.

Apparently that implied we were a thruple.
I was unaware.
They were not.

Probation lasted longer than expected.
Six more months.
Direct route to work only.
No stops for gas.
No detours.
No fun.
Eventually I returned home.
James admitted he was bored without my chaos.
Imagine that.

I once tried to escort un unaccompanied visitor out of the building for not wearing a badge.
She was the new HR supervisor.
We laughed about that for years.

Then came the technical lead who locked doors with young female agents.
I reported him.
He was suspended.
Later, corporate accused me of falsifying his review.
They produced a glowing appraisal.
I turned red.
I nearly cried.
But HR walked with me to my desk.

We found my signed copy.
The real one.
It saved my job.
Sometimes righteousness needs receipts.

CHAPTER THIRTY-FOUR

On a snowy corporate trip, the roads were a mess and the parking lot looked like a skating rink. On the way to the dinner gala, I stopped and bought a pair of men's black socks. My shoes were already damp, and I figured if my feet got soaked later, I'd at least have a backup plan. The socks went into my purse with the rest of my questionable life decisions.

Inside the ballroom I was seated with a rowdy table of television repair technicians who treated the gala like a tailgate party.

Next to me sat a quiet man in a suit.

At one point he mentioned, almost apologetically, that his feet were cold and wet from the snow.

Well.

That sounded like a problem I could solve.

I reached into my purse, pulled out the brand-new socks, slid under the table, removed his shoes, and replaced his damp socks with dry ones.

When I popped back up, the entire table was staring.

I calmly sealed his wet socks in a Ziploc bag from my purse and continued eating dinner.

A little later someone stepped to the microphone.

The keynote speaker for the evening.

The man whose feet I had just socked.

Vice President.

My turn to be shocked.

During his speech he told the room about the woman at his table who climbed under it to rescue his frozen feet with spare socks.

The room erupted in laughter.

Then applause.

All because I had spare socks.

And a mouth that doesn't stay quiet.

When I returned to work two days later, I went straight to my director's office with a freshly laundered pair of men's socks in my hand.

"I need you to return these to the Vice President," I said sheepishly.

He stared at the socks. Then at me.

Then he burst into laughter.

"Oh, I've already heard about the impact you made at headquarters. I swear, I can't send you anywhere without adult supervision. Should I go ahead and reserve a conference room in HR now?"

I smiled sweetly.

"Probably."

There was an older woman on my team who proudly identified as Wiccan.

She had crystals on her desk. Stones she said were blessed. She read palms during lunch and occasionally offered to curse people on request.

I let her have her books.

Just like others had Bibles.

But I pulled her aside one day and said gently:

"You can believe whatever you want. But no proselytizing at work."

She nodded.

The next morning, I stopped by her desk and noticed what looked like a Southern women's cookbook.

It was not.

It was a spell book disguised as a cookbook.

At lunch, she ran up to me — breathless — and handed me a jar filled with screws, thumbtacks, nails, and razor blades.

"Pee in this," she whispered urgently. "Seal it tight. Bury it in the northwest corner of your yard during the full moon. It's been blessed by my High Warlock. It will protect you from your evil manager."

My manager happened to be standing next to me.

He jumped back like he'd seen an apparition.

I stared at the jar.

Then at her.

Then at him.

There are moments in life when you realize you cannot possibly be making this up.

This was one of them.

A few months later, I was sent to Jamaica to help open a new call center.

One week, they said.

I packed for two.

If I'm going to train people to replace my team, I might as well do it well.

The young people there were bright. Hungry. Funny.

And I have never believed outsourcing should be miserable.

So I decided we'd celebrate Carnivale.

Four dollars for unlimited rum punch.

Company bus provided.

James gave his blessing.

The warm air, the music, the laughter — I loved every second.

We went again Friday night.

Casino.

Bottle service.

Pizza at sunrise.

The young men told me they wanted to repay me with something special.

"We'll take you to chuch," they said.

Chuch.

I woke Sunday morning, put on a black suit and white blouse. I even grabbed a lace doily from under a plant and pinned it to my head. Preacher's daughter muscle memory.

They forgot me at noon.

I almost cried.

Then at 11 p.m., the concierge called.

"A bus full of young men is here for you."

Midnight mass, I assumed.

I put the doily back on.

Grabbed the Gideon Bible.

I was wrong.

They took me to what had once been a cathedral.

There was a sign outside that read "tithes."

Two dollars per person.

I paid.

Inside, the pews were full.

Mostly men.

Spotlights hit.

Music exploded.

Women rushed the stage, glittering, gyrating, ascending poles like acrobatic angels.

I clutched my Bible.

And my pearls.

I had never been inside a fully nude gentlemen's club.

I also had never been "baptized" in champagne before.

Yes.

That happened.

When the Master of Ceremonies poured champagne over four women and they arched and sprayed the front rows in synchronized display, he declared we had been "formally baptized."

I sat there, slightly damp, slightly stunned.

And very aware that I was absolutely not in Kansas anymore.

The first dancer leapt into my lap.

I froze.

Then instinct kicked in.

I wrapped my arms around her and massaged her shoulders.

She melted.

Apparently, word traveled.

Because nine women lined up for "the red-headed American massage."

One even offered me money for a more intimate service.

I declined.

But I laughed.

The irony was not lost on me:

Nine lap dances.

Bible crushed between us.

Men whining that I got all the attention.

Sometimes you cannot write irony this rich.

I accidentally walked into a former nursing room where men stood facing the stage with their trousers down.

I backed out quickly.

I found a door that once read "Prayer Room."

The "R" had been crossed out.
It now read "Pay'er Room."
Security stood guard.
I understood.
I giggled.
I have always processed shock with humor.

We closed the place down at 5 a.m.
Two hours later I was at work.
The young men winked at me all day.
Bowed occasionally.
I decided Jamaica had the most creative definition of "church"
I'd ever seen.

When I returned to the States, my own team had been laid off
while I was away.
That part hurt.
The fun.
The chaos.
The wild nights.
They always sit next to loss.

One morning on my drive to work, something felt off.
Cars were unusually polite.
People waved.
Moved over.
Let me pass.

I cranked Linkin Park and sang at the top of my lungs.
Felt free.
Alone on the interstate.
Wind in my hair.
Music loud.
Life wide open.
And I thought:
Everything feels perfect.
Which, as I've learned,
is usually when the curtain starts to tremble

CHAPTER THIRTY-FIVE

I was driving across the high-rise bridge when the world blinked.

That's the only way I know how to explain it.

One second I was singing.

The next second, nothing.

I lost consciousness at the apex of the bridge.

Apparently, my right foot slipped off the gas pedal and the car — still moving at forty-five miles per hour — drifted down the incline like it had a mind of its own. It scraped one side of the guardrail, then the other. Drivers behind me had already called highway patrol because they'd noticed the erratic weaving before I went out completely.

The car eventually drifted into a grassy shoulder and came to a stop.

When I came to, there were flashing lights.

An ambulance.

Concerned faces.

And adrenaline.

I felt fine.

So I declined the ride to the emergency room.

I drove to work.

Of course I did.

By the time I parked, my right leg felt heavy.

Not painful.

Just… not mine.

I tried to push the building door open.

My right arm didn't respond.

Security opened it for me.
Inside, the director stood in the breakroom.
"Good morning," he said.
I opened my mouth to answer.
Nothing came out.
No words.
No sound.
Just air.
I remember the look on his face.
And then hands grabbing me.
Sirens again.

At the hospital, the nurse asked me what day it was.
I couldn't answer.
She asked what color the curtain was.
I wrote down pink and blue.
It was green and yellow.
My mouth felt wrong.
My thoughts felt scrambled.
My body wasn't listening.
They said I needed to be admitted.
But the hospital was over an hour from home.
And I am stubborn.
So I left.
Without permission.
I had a friend drive me to a hospital closer to home.
On the way there, she later told me, I sounded drunk.
Gibberish.
Slurred.
Laughing at nothing.
I don't remember that part.

Late that night, I remembered something essential.
I had a husband.
I scratched a note for my friend:
Call James.
He arrived pale.
Angry.
Scared.
Both.

The scans showed brain injury.
A stroke.
The neurosurgeon explained which areas were damaged.
They did a spinal tap.
More tests.
More words.
Then the verdict:
I could no longer do math.
Not complicated math.
Not basic math.
Not even counting past three.
Numbers on a page triggered panic so severe I couldn't breathe.
Speech therapy.
Motor therapy.
Physical therapy.
Twice a week.
For months.
I had panic attacks in the car on the way to therapy.
Screaming.
Thrashing.
Trying to claw my way out of the passenger seat.
I didn't understand why.

But my body did.

Numbers.

Speed.

Bridges.

My nervous system had decided it had had enough.

Depression came quietly.

James propped me upright on the couch with pillows when he left for work.

A neighbor came by every few hours to check on me.

I couldn't calculate change.

Couldn't write clearly.

Couldn't trust my right hand.

I — the woman who outran storms, corporations, judges, and vice presidents — could not count to four.

The neurosurgeon sent me to a psychiatrist.

I still couldn't speak clearly.

So I wrote.

Pages and pages of responses.

James spoke when I couldn't.

"She's always been a risk-taker," he said.

"A rabble-rouser."

"She never stops moving."

"She never stops talking."

He didn't know how to care for someone who suddenly… stopped.

The psychiatrist listened.

Wrote something on a prescription pad.

137

Tore the paper.
Handed it to James.
We went to the pharmacy.
The drive-through line wrapped around the building.
James wouldn't leave me alone in the car.
We waited.
And waited.
When we reached the window, he handed over the prescription.
The clerk stared at it.
Called a supervisor.
Then the pharmacist.
All three looked at James.
He was already on edge.
"What's wrong with it?" he demanded.
They slid the paper back through the tray.
"Did you read it?" the clerk asked.
James turned it over.
It read:
GO ON A CRUISE.
No medication.
No sedative.
No antidepressant.
Just that.
Go.
On.
A.
Cruise.
I stared at the words.
And for the first time since the bridge,
I laughed.
Not hysterically.
Not wildly.
Just softly.

Because apparently,
when you outrun everything long enough,
your brain shuts the curtain itself.
And sometimes,
the prescription
isn't to fight.
It's to float.

CHAPTER THIRTY-SIX

When we got home from the pharmacy and realized my official medical treatment plan was "Go on a cruise," James and I just stood there staring at each other.

No pills.

No injections.

No miracle brain potion.

Just salt water and a ship.

We figured, why not?

I couldn't talk.

I couldn't walk right.

I couldn't count past three without spiraling into panic.

What else did we have to lose?

We started looking up cruises leaving from the East Coast.

Cheap ones.

Nothing fancy.

We weren't chasing luxury.

We were chasing relief.

Life kept life-ing in the meantime.

Therapy twice a week.

Specialists.

Exercises.

James missing work.

Me staring at walls.

Trying to say words that came out sounding like static.

I was trapped inside my own mouth.

And then, because apparently the universe wasn't done humbling me, I had a knee replacement.

Now I couldn't talk and I couldn't walk.

Stellar.

By cruise day, I rolled onto that ship in a wheelchair like a woman who had lived three lifetimes and lost all three.

At dinner, James explained to the table that I couldn't really speak but I loved funny stories.

He invited strangers to tell me about their kids doing ridiculous things, pranks they'd pulled, dumb decisions they'd survived.

They talked.

I listened.

For the first time since the stroke, my brain wasn't fighting.

It wasn't calculating.

It wasn't panicking.

It wasn't trying to outrun anything.

It was just… enjoying.

After dinner, James wanted to play poker.

The man looked at me like I was a fragile package he didn't know where to set down.

He hoisted me onto a stool at a slot machine and loaded money onto my card.

I couldn't do math.

I couldn't balance a checkbook.

I couldn't count the steps to the elevator without my chest tightening.

But a slot machine?

Push a button.
Lights flash.
Coins dance.
Possibility.
No arithmetic required.
Even my scrambled brain could handle that.

I smoked.
I sipped Long Island iced teas.
I hit the button.
And I kept hitting it.
The noise, the lights, the repetition — it was like my brain found a rhythm again.
No one expected anything from me there.
No one needed me to be funny or fast or dangerous.
I just existed in the glow.

By the end of the cruise, I had won enough bonuses to play the entire week.
When we disembarked, I got a letter.
Apparently, I was now a "VIP Whale."
Free balcony cabin next cruise.
Free drinks.
Five hundred dollars in casino credit.
I had gone from stroke victim to high-roller in five days.
Tell me God doesn't have a sense of humor.

We cruised again.
And again.
And again.
Five more times. All free.
By the fifth cruise, I was talking clearer.
Walking better.
Laughing easier.
The panic around numbers had softened.
The gibberish had turned back into sentences.
My psychiatrist had been right.
The ocean did what medicine couldn't.

On every cruise after that, James would wheel me to the smoking section before heading off on his excursions.

I'd sit with retired military veterans and ask them to tell me stories.

War stories.

Love stories.

Stories about being young and stupid and surviving anyway.

And I would listen.

That's when I understood something.
For years, I thought escalation was oxygen.
If it wasn't louder or closer to the edge, I lost interest.
I pushed rooms.
Men.
Rules.
Myself.
I thought rebellion was freedom.

Turns out, rebellion without reflection is just noise.

Sitting there in the smoke and salt air, something stopped fighting inside me.

For years I treated Scarlett and George like opposing forces — preacher's daughter on one side, chaos conductor on the other.

I blamed George for the flirting.

The risk-taking.

The urge to light something just to see who ran.

But they were never rivals.

They were the same woman moving through different rooms.

The believer who memorized Scripture and the one who kept handcuffs in a desk drawer weren't contradictions.

They were context.

The stroke stripped the noise away.

The ocean gave me room to hear what remained.

I wasn't fractured.

I was whole.

CHAPTER THIRTY-SEVEN

On one of those cruises, while parked at the casino bar with a cigarette balanced between my fingers, I met a tall, broad-shouldered butch lesbian who introduced herself without blinking as Secret Lover.

Now you don't ignore a name like that.

James didn't.

Secret Lover owned a ranch in Texas and rescued abandoned dogs.

That combination of grit and tenderness?

It hooked me instantly.

There were thousands of people floating on that ship, but somehow the three of us locked into a gravitational pull.

By the second night, we were inseparable.

We set up camp at a Heidi slot machine.

Every time I hit a bonus, German Heidi burst onto the screen, bouncing and scattering jewels theatrically from her exaggerated chest.

It was absurd.

It was shameless.

It was magnificent.

James and Secret Lover hovered over my shoulders like conspirators waiting for ignition.

When the bonus music hit, they would both start shimmying on either side of the machine — hips rolling, shoulders shaking, hands on the chrome — like they were auditioning for a very inappropriate church revival.

People gathered.

They cheered.

They fed my machine like we were summoning a deity.

At one point, I had a semicircle of onlookers chanting for Heidi to "bounce again."

Secret Lover leaned over and whispered in my ear that if those animated jewels kept flying, she might need a moment alone.

James nearly fell over laughing.

It became ritual.

I'd sit between them like a queen holding court.

They'd call me wifey.

I'd call them hubby.

We didn't explain ourselves.

We didn't clarify dynamics.

We let people wonder.

When someone finally asked if we were together, Secret Lover didn't hesitate.

"Hell yeah," she said, draping an arm across both of us with territorial pride.

If they pushed further, I'd toss my hair and answer, "Utah. We're a family."

The way people grabbed their children and backed away?

Delicious.

It wasn't about scandal.

It wasn't about being shocking for shock's sake.

It was about owning the room.

About knowing the power of suggestion.

About understanding that confidence — real, embodied confidence — makes people uncomfortable when they can't categorize you.

And I loved that.

Before we parted at the end of the cruise, Secret Lover lifted her drink and announced loudly enough for half the bar to hear,

"Whichever one of you dies first, don't worry. I'll marry the other."

James sputtered.

I grinned.

In that moment, I wasn't chasing chaos or trying to escalate anything.

I wasn't staging rebellion.

I was just there.

That's not the same thing.

CHAPTER THIRTY-EIGHT

Apparently three-quarters of that cruise ship was drunk before sunset every day.

By nightfall?

It was a floating reality show.

Fistfights broke out nightly.

Security ran laps.

Glass shattered.

It was festive in a concerning way.

One evening, while waiting for James and Secret Lover to join me, I parked myself at a slot machine between an older married couple.

The husband was already deep into his own apocalypse.

He slammed the buttons like the machine had insulted his ancestors.

In one hand, he clutched a full bottle of wine and drank from it like hydration was optional.

He growled.

He splashed me.

He missed the button entirely at least five times.

Then he finished the bottle, flung it across the room like a Viking offering, and passed out.

I leaned over to check if he was breathing.

He responded by releasing a sound so violent and barnyard-level that I briefly considered calling Animal Control.

His wife?

Never stopped pressing the spin button.

I alerted the bartender.

He glanced over and shrugged.

"Him? He's a regular. He'll wake up."

Floating humanity.

I tell you.

Disembarkation morning was even better.

James and I were in the first wave off the ship when I noticed police cruisers lining the port.

One after another.

Twelve at least.

Paddy wagons too.

Then came the parade — twenty handcuffed men escorted off like they'd mistaken the cruise for Fight Club at Sea.

James asked security if this was unusual.

The guard laughed.

"No ma'am. They get banned for fighting. Spend the year saving. Come back. Fight again."

Commitment is commitment.

Secret Lover and I hugged goodbye.

James hugged too.

We promised to keep in touch.

Friends for life.

Or… something adjacent.

A few cruises later, somewhere over the Atlantic, I felt a filling pop out of my back tooth.

No problem.

I pressed it back into place with my tongue like a responsible adult.

It fit perfectly.

Crisis managed.

Or so I thought.

By dinner, my jaw throbbed.

I chewed on the other side and pretended nothing was wrong.

By midnight, the left side of my face had swollen to cartoon villain proportions.

When I looked in the mirror, one eye was nearly shut.

I visited the ship's medical facility hoping for a dentist.

What I got was a man with bare hands and a bottle of Vicodin.

He scooped pills like trail mix and placed them into a tiny envelope.

"You pain?" he asked.

I nodded vigorously.

I wrote:

Where are your gloves? This is not sanitary. I need antibiotics.

He opened a drawer and produced a single wrinkled latex glove that looked like it had survived three previous lifetimes.

It had a paperclip holding it closed.

There were pencil shavings on it.

I chose infection over whatever that glove had seen.

Eventually I left with mystery antibiotics crushed into powder because I couldn't open my mouth wide enough to swallow them whole.

And then?

The real entertainment began.

As I walked the promenade, people recoiled.

Parents grabbed their children.

Whispers followed me like wind.

James walked slightly behind me, pretending we were acquaintances.

I looked like the Beast.

The unsymmetrical, slightly infected version.

And then I realized:

If they were going to clear a path…

I might as well use it.

Breakfast buffet? Empty.

Casino? Vacated in under thirty seconds.

I stood near my favorite slot machines and watched three players slowly clock my swollen face.

One squealed.

Another cashed out.

The third practically fled.

James and I had prime casino real estate for hours.

Straws became essential.

Vodka cranberries numbed everything.

For a few hours at a time, I forgot I resembled a maritime cautionary tale.

After five days of hiding on the ship, I demanded land.

We docked.

I stood in line.

My badge was scanned.

An alarm sounded.

The crew member's screen flashed red.

QUARANTINED — INFECTIOUS DISEASE — MUMPS

Mumps.

I didn't even know anyone still got mumps.

I wasn't allowed off the ship.

Worse?

I was confined to my cabin for the final three days.

Meals were delivered to my door:

Yogurt.

Mashed potatoes.

Peanut butter.

No alcohol.

Now that felt punitive.

I sat in that cabin staring at my swollen reflection in the mirror.

One eye half-closed.

Jaw distorted.

Hair wild.

Pride dented.

Of all the ways I've tried to make an entrance or an exit in life…

I did not expect quarantine.

But here's the part I don't tell as loudly.

There is something humbling about being confined.

About not being able to perform.

About having no audience to shock, no crowd to part, no machine to conquer.

For three days, the ship moved without me.

The casino spun without me.
The buffet opened without me.
The world did not need my disruption.
And I had nowhere to go.
No one recoiling.
No one applauding.
No one watching.
Just me.
My crooked smile.
My stubborn pulse.
My swollen face.
Still here.
Still breathing.
Still… me.

I've spent a lifetime pushing rooms to see if they would move.
Testing edges.
Escalating the climb.
Quarantine didn't scare me.
It silenced me.
And in that silence, something unfamiliar happened.
I wasn't bored.
I wasn't restless.
I wasn't plotting.
I was… still.
Not punished.
Recalibrated.

Maybe that's what this whole season has been.

Not slowing down.

Not shutting up.

But finally finding a center that doesn't require chaos to feel alive.

Even the Beast eventually returns to herself.

And when the cabin door finally opened?

I didn't rush out.

I stood.

Adjusted my crown.

And walked.

CHAPTER THIRTY-NINE

The swollen-face quarantine turned out to be an expensive lesson.

When I got home, I was put on major antibiotics. A week later, the tooth had to be pulled.

I recovered — eventually.

But cruising and my teeth apparently had an agreement I wasn't aware of.

On another cruise, a crown popped off while I was flossing.

A year later, I lost a filling.

On yet another, I cracked a molar biting into a crab leg like I was trying to prove something.

At that point my dentist and I made a pact: one month before every cruise, I sit in his chair and let him inspect every inch of my mouth like we're preparing for battle.

Fifteen years and thirty-four cruises later, I still report for pre-sailing dental clearance.

Lessons learned.

My best friend — a lifelong learner in every sense — had always refused to cruise with us.

Classes. Certifications. Seminars. Always something.

When a deeply discounted sailing came along, she finally agreed.

She trusted me to make sure she had fun.

That was her first mistake.

For three solid years, she and I had gone to TGI Friday's after work every single night. Long Islands. Appetizers. Co-workers rotating in and out.

On nights it was just the two of us, I'd excuse myself, walk up to a lone man at the bar, and say:

"See that woman with the long red hair? She looks lonely. Would you mind sitting with her and buying her a drink?"

She's shy. Quiet. Doesn't love attention.

I adore attention.

After a few free drinks, she'd loosen up and laugh. She now says she deserves a medal for surviving our friendship.

On the cruise, James ordered her something called a fish bowl — four sixteen-ounce drinks in one glass.

She and James played trivia and cards while I handled my professional responsibilities in the casino.

Three days at sea before the first port.

By day three she said she felt confined. Claustrophobic.

James looked out the porthole toward the distant lights of Cuba and said calmly,

"If you want off the ship, just step over the side. Hope you can swim."

She stopped complaining.

I continued introducing her to eligible strangers.

One sailing took us directly alongside a tropical storm that turned into a hurricane.

Seventy-knot winds.

Security stationed at every outside door.

Barf bags at every elevator.

On Deck Five, we sat facing massive windows. One moment: sky. The next: nothing but water.

People were locked in their cabins, seasick and pale.

James and I were hungry.

The buffet had exactly one station open. One man stood at the counter, frozen, plate in hand, staring into space.

James walked up slowly behind him.

"You can really feel the ship going UP and DOWN up here on the Lido deck," he said gently.

The man turned red, dropped his plate, and sprinted for the nearest restroom.

The crew member behind the counter leaned over and whispered,

"I see what you did."

We were monsters.

Later, James discovered if he timed it right, he could run up a staircase just as the ship dipped and become briefly weightless.

Children gathered.

He'd yell "GO!" and a pack of them would fly upward in slow-motion joy.

A woman approached me.

"Which one is yours?"

"The tall one," I said proudly.

The storm damaged our Florida port. We were held at sea an extra day.

Rumors flew that the city had evacuated inland.

The next morning, three massive cruise ships anchored side by side — over nine thousand passengers waiting to disembark at once.

Mayhem.

We got off at 10:30 a.m. and waited until 3:30 p.m. for a bus.

Our flight was canceled. Our home airport shut down.

We were stranded in Orlando for four days.

My daughter pulled strings through SeaWorld connections and secured us a hotel room when the entire city was "sold out."

VIP suite.

Laundry done.

SeaWorld passes secured.

And then James had an idea.

"If SeaWorld gives temporary passes," he said thoughtfully, "shouldn't Disney?"

Two days later we were at EPCOT during Food & Wine Festival, eating and drinking our way around the world like displaced royalty.

When we finally got home, James called cruise insurance.

Every single dollar reimbursed.

Always get cruise insurance.

And here's what I've learned.

Storms don't scare me.

Quarantine doesn't stop me.

Teeth betray me — repeatedly.

But I adapt.

I find the open buffet.

I find the loophole.

I find the VIP suite.

I find the free drinks.

Cruising didn't just recalibrate me.

It taught me that no matter how violently the ship rocks, I can still stand upright — or at least laugh while sliding sideways.

And if I can't dock where I planned,

I'll find another port.

CHAPTER FORTY

After about five years of cruising, my words came back.

Not all at once. Not perfectly. But fluently enough. Clearly enough. Confidently enough.

And once I could speak again?

Oh, I spoke.

I started telling funny Scarlett stories to anyone sitting alone. Small clusters in the smoking section. Strangers at dinner tables. People sipping fruity drinks with umbrellas who looked like they needed something more than sunburn and buffet lines.

I loved watching laughter hit them in waves.

Telling my stories helped me make friends fast. I'd start with something light — a cruise mishap, a James moment, a small rebellion — and within minutes chairs would start scraping closer.

People would lean in.

Then someone else would stop and ask, "What happened next?"

Before long, a small group would gather. Fifteen. Twenty. Sometimes more. Curious faces wondering why everyone was laughing so hard.

That's when I'd go deeper.

Philippines.

Jamaica.

Black markets.

Near arrests.

Massages in churches that weren't churches.

Shock. Awe. Timing.

No one would leave for the buffet. No one would check their phones. They hung on every word like I was handing out oxygen.

And I felt it.

The rhythm.

The pause.

The lean-in moment.

The room moving with me.

One cruise, about seven years after my stroke, the ship had only one outdoor smoking section.

The regulars found each other quickly — morning coffee smokers, late-night bourbon smokers, the lifers.

We became a tribe.

One afternoon, James nudged me.

"Tell them a story."

There were nearly thirty people gathered around the deck chairs, ashtrays full, drinks sweating in their hands.

I started with the Manila black market.

The pomp and circumstance.

The elephant door handle.

The Turkish palace room.

The preacher's daughter moment.

It took over thirty minutes to tell it right.

No one moved.

Not one person stood up.

When I finished, someone shouted, "Another one!"

So I told Jamaica.

Then I told another.

By the time I stopped, it was well past lunch. I was starving. The sun had shifted overhead. My drink was warm.

But nobody left.

More chairs were dragged over. Smokers. Non-smokers. People just passing by who heard laughter and curiosity and decided to stay.

I wasn't just telling stories.

I was holding a room.

And something clicked inside me.

Cruising hadn't just helped me recover.

It had given me a stage without walls.

No spotlight.

No microphone.

Just air, salt, smoke, and strangers who didn't know they needed me.

For years I had been pushing rooms — testing edges, escalating risk, climbing staircases just to see how high they went.

Now?

I didn't have to push.

People leaned in.

I had found something I didn't even know I'd been searching for.

I used to think it had to be louder. Riskier. Edgier.

If it didn't flirt with danger, I lost interest.

But what held that deck together wasn't rebellion. It wasn't shock value. And it definitely wasn't chaos.

It was presence.

For years I climbed staircases just to see how far they went.

This time, I wasn't climbing.

I had finally stood still long enough to notice I wasn't at the bottom anymore.

And somehow, they were still listening.

CHAPTER FORTY-ONE

By the fourth morning in the smoking section, I had become
something of a cruise attraction.

People drifted in and out of the chairs facing the sea. Drinks
sweating in their hands. Cigarettes burning down to filters because
they forgot to ash.

What started as one story turned into six. Then six became
ritual.

Every time new listeners joined the circle, June would tilt her
head slightly and say,

"Tell the Manila one again."

I'd laugh.

"Y'all sure you want to hear it again?"

They always did.

June sat quietly every time — back straight, hands folded, long
dreadlocks falling like a royal mantle over her shoulders.

She didn't interrupt. She didn't embellish.

She simply listened. Studied. Absorbed.

By formal night, I had told half my life story to a crowd that no
longer felt like strangers.

After dinner and the musical review, James and I returned to the
smoking deck. The regulars were already there.

The ocean was black velvet. The ship hummed steady beneath
our feet.

June stood.

"I'd like to invite everyone to the comedy show tonight."

Cheers. Whistles. Applause.

It wasn't until we were escorted to reserved balcony seating that I understood.

Our quiet, stately June wasn't just a fellow cruiser.

She was the headliner.

The lights dimmed.

Applause rolled through the theater as she walked onto the stage.

"Good evening," she began. "I had a prepared set for tonight… but I've decided to do something different."

James' hand tightened around mine.

"For the past several days, I've been listening to stories from a fellow passenger. Stories so outrageous, so inappropriate, so unbelievable… that I can't improve on them."

The smoking section erupted.

"Tonight," June smiled, "I'm telling what we now call Scarlett Stories."

For forty minutes, I heard my life delivered with precision.

The Manila black market.

Jamaica's 'chuch.'

Lap dances.

The stroke.

The cruise prescription.

The timing was flawless. The pauses were surgical.

The punchlines landed harder than I ever dared to land them myself.

People gasped. People cried laughing. People wiped tears.

But she didn't mock the stories.
She honored them.
She let the chaos breathe.

And hearing my life through someone else's voice did something to me I didn't expect.
It wasn't just trouble.
It wasn't recklessness.
It wasn't "too much."
It was timing.
It was nerve.
It was survival wrapped in absurdity.
It was art.

When June finished, the audience was on its feet.
But she wasn't done.
She asked members of each military branch to stand.
Applause thundered.
First responders stood next.
More applause.
Then she paused.
"And now… I'd like James to stand."
James shook his head immediately. Mortified.
A spotlight found him anyway.
He rose slowly.
June pointed toward him.
"We've applauded bravery tonight. But I want you to give a standing ovation to the man who has put up with this woman's

nonsense for over forty years. He is either a saint... or the bravest man on this ship."

The audience roared.

James stood there, red-faced and stunned, as hundreds of strangers clapped for him.

For the first time in decades, he wasn't just my husband.

He was James.

People lined up afterward for selfies with him. They shook his hand. Thanked him. Congratulated him.

I watched it all — proud, amused, unexpectedly tender.

I had always been the spectacle.

That night, James became the headline.

And it didn't threaten me.

It completed me.

Because somewhere between the smoking section and the spotlight, I realized something else.

I wasn't performing anymore.

I was sharing.

And there's a difference.

CHAPTER FORTY-TWO

People love the stories.

They lean in for the chaos — the strip clubs disguised as churches, the quarantines, the hurricanes, the slot machines, the lap dances, the champagne baptisms.

They especially love when I grin and say,

"You can call me Trouble."

What I don't always say is this:

The stroke terrified me.

Not the drifting car.

Not the ambulance ride.

The silence.

The morning I couldn't count past three. The afternoon numbers crawled across the page like insects. The moment I opened my mouth and nothing followed.

For someone who had talked her way into — and out of — nearly everything, losing language felt like suffocating slowly.

I was furious.

At my body.

At the fragility of it.

At needing James to steady me like something breakable.

I hated that I couldn't walk without help. That the woman who once ran departments now struggled with a fork.

And underneath that anger was something quieter.

Fear.

Fear that James would tire of caretaking. Fear that I had already used up whatever luck had been assigned to me. Fear that the stories — the only currency I trusted — were finished.

The psychiatrist didn't offer pills.

She offered movement.

"Go on a cruise."

At the time it sounded ridiculous. Like prescribing champagne for a concussion.

But somewhere between salt air and strangers laughing at things that barely made sense, something shifted.

I wasn't stirring trouble because I was reckless.

I was restless.

Stillness felt like disappearance.

If I kept the room laughing, maybe no one would see the parts of me that were shaking.

Cruising didn't repair my brain.

Time did.

Therapy did.

James did.

But the ocean reminded me that my voice hadn't left.

It had simply changed shape.

And crooked can still carry weight.

Now, when someone says, "Tell us another one," I hear something I missed when I was younger.

It was never really about the chaos.

It was about the circle.

The chairs pulled close.

The strangers who stay.

The husband who never walked away.

James and I are retired now.

We drive our golf cart to potlucks and community dances.

I still introduce myself the same way

"My name's Scarlett. You can call me Trouble."

James laughs. Shakes his head.

"She means it."

I do.

I don't stir trouble just to feel alive anymore.

I write it down.

Because stories like mine don't end.
They just wait for their next chapter.

FINAL CONFESSIONS

You've probably been wondering whether any of this actually happened.

The strip clubs called churches.

The quarantines.

The hurricanes.

The shark excursion.

The black markets.

The psychiatrist who wrote, "Go on a cruise."

It did.

Every scene. Every memory. Every uncomfortable detail.

Some edges were softened — not to deceive you, but because not everything belongs to public consumption.

Other moments remain exactly as they were.

Leaving them out would have been the lie.

But whether you believe every word isn't what matters most.

What matters is what happened inside you while you were reading.

Did you laugh?

Did you flinch?

Did you judge me and then recognize something uncomfortably familiar?

That's where the truth lives.

I've spent most of my life stepping into the spotlight — not because I needed applause, but because I refused to sit quietly and watch it pass by.

The better question isn't whether my stories are real.

It's whether you're living yours.

Are you stepping forward?

Or are you still waiting for someone to tell you it's safe?

If you decide to write your own confessions — the messy ones, the sacred ones, the parts you don't read aloud at church — I hope you do it without trimming the edges that make you human.

Maybe I'll see you somewhere unexpected.

Maybe on a cruise ship.

Pull up a chair. Order something strong.

Tell me where you almost went under.

Tell me how you surfaced.

We'll trade stories.

No stage required.

— Scarlett

———— 🍂 ————

The end?

No, just the beginning.

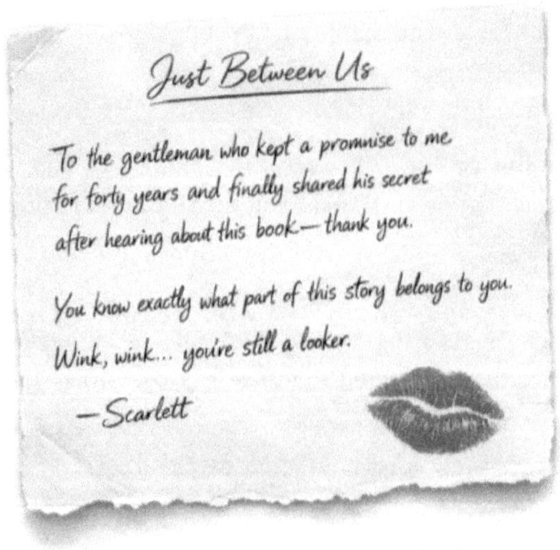

A NOTE TO BOOK CLUBS

If you're reading this book with a group of people sitting around someone's living room, passing snacks, refilling drinks, and occasionally interrupting each other to say, "Wait—did she really?"…

First of all, I'm honored you invited me into the room.

When I started telling these stories, it was never about writing a book. It was about conversation. About people pulling their chairs closer and laughing so hard they forgot what time it was.

That's how most of these stories were originally told — on cruise ship decks, in smoky corners, and around tables with strangers who quickly stopped feeling like strangers.

If this book did its job, you probably found yourself reacting in different ways.

Maybe you laughed.

Maybe you shook your head and thought, "This woman is out of her mind."

Maybe a few moments made you uncomfortable.

That's okay.

Life is messy, and the truth usually shows up somewhere between the laughter and the raised eyebrows.

So as you talk about the book together, don't worry about getting the "right" answers to the discussion questions.

Instead, talk about the things that stuck with you.

The moment you recognized yourself.

The story that reminded you of someone you love.

Or the part that made you wonder if you've been playing life a little safer than you really want to.

If the conversation wanders, let it wander.

That's usually where the best stories live.

— Scarlett

READER REFLECTION

Your Turn

By the time you reached the end of this book, you've heard plenty about my adventures — the chaos, the mistakes, the storms, the near disasters, and the strange ways life sometimes puts us back together again.

But the real question isn't whether you believe my stories. It's whether you've been paying attention to your own. So, take a moment and think about a few things.

1. Where in your life have you stirred a little trouble?
2. Was it a decision people warned you about?
   a) A risk you took that turned into a story?
   b) A moment when you surprised yourself?
3. When did life force you to recalibrate?
4. Maybe it was a health scare.
   a) A loss.
   b) A job that ended.
   c) A relationship that changed.
5. What did you learn about yourself when everything slowed down?
6. Who has been your "James"? The person who stayed steady while life got loud. The one who didn't walk away when things got messy.

And finally…

7. If someone pulled up a chair and said, "Tell me where you almost went under." What story would you tell? Because somewhere out there, someone else probably needs to hear it. And you never know. Your story might be the one that makes the whole room lean in.

BOOK CLUB DISCUSSION QUESTIONS

1. Scarlett often introduces herself by saying, "You can call me Trouble." Is trouble something she causes… or something she refuses to run from?

2. The book is filled with outrageous stories — strip clubs called churches, hurricanes at sea, lap dances, and black markets. Which moment made you laugh the hardest, and which moment made you pause?

3. Scarlett suggests that chaos and storytelling are connected. Do you think people who live boldly naturally become storytellers, or do storytellers simply notice life more?

4. One of the turning points in the memoir is the stroke that takes away Scarlett's ability to speak and even count past three. How did this moment change your understanding of the earlier "Trouble" stories?

5. The psychiatrist's prescription — "Go on a cruise" — sounds ridiculous at first. Have you ever received advice that seemed absurd but later turned out to be exactly what you needed?

6. Scarlett wrestles with two sides of herself: the preacher's daughter and the chaos-loving rebel. Do you think those identities conflict, or do they actually complement each other?

7. For readers with a religious background: How did Scarlett's upbringing shape her understanding of risk, morality, and forgiveness?

8. For readers without a religious background: Did Scarlett's spiritual roots make you see her choices differently?

9. The book asks an interesting question: Is rebellion always rebellion, or can it sometimes be curiosity? Where do you think Scarlett falls on that spectrum?

10. Throughout the memoir, James remains steady while Scarlett creates whirlwinds. What role do you think he plays in the story — anchor, witness, partner in crime, or something else?

11. Scarlett fears that after the stroke she might lose the one thing she trusted most: her ability to tell stories. Have you ever worried about losing a skill or identity that defined you?

12. Many of the funniest moments in the book happen in places where things could have gone terribly wrong. Why do you think humor shows up so often in Scarlett's life?

13. The cruise ships become more than vacations — they become classrooms, stages, and therapy sessions. Why do you think strangers were willing to gather around and listen to her stories?

14. Scarlett eventually realizes she isn't performing anymore — she's sharing. What do you think the difference is?

15. The memoir repeatedly returns to the idea of recalibration rather than reinvention. Do you think people truly reinvent themselves, or do they simply rediscover who they were all along?

16. Scarlett writes that "crooked can still carry weight." What does that line mean to you?

17. Several readers say the book made them examine their own lives while laughing at Scarlett's. Did you find yourself reflecting on your own risks, regrets, or wild stories?

18. Scarlett suggests that people often wait for permission before living boldly. Do you think that's true?

19. If you met Scarlett in the cruise ship smoking section and
    she said, "Tell me where you almost went under," what story
    would you tell her?
20. After finishing the book, do you think Scarlett is still
    "Trouble"? Or has she become something else entirely?

BONUS QUESTIONS

Scarlett Would Approve

If you had to spend one week on a cruise ship with Scarlett, which of these would you most hope to experience?

1. A hurricane at sea
2. A comedy show about your life
3. A casino night that gets out of hand
4. A philosophical conversation at 2 a.m.
5. All of the above (plus bail money)

Explain your answer.

____

____

____

____

____

____

____

____

____

____

____

____

____

____

____

SCARLETT'S RULES FOR SURVIVING LIFE

As observed somewhere between a hurricane, a cruise ship,
and a psychiatric prescription

1. If a psychiatrist writes "Go on a cruise," don't argue. Pack
    sunscreen.
2. If the room gets quiet when you walk in, sit down and tell a
    story.
    Silence is just an audience waiting for instructions.
3. When the ship rocks, bend your knees and laugh.
    Life rarely asks if you're ready.
4. Always marry someone who can laugh at you publicly and
    love you privately.
5. If people are leaning in, keep talking.
    If they're leaning back… you might have gone too far. Or you
    might be getting interesting.
6. Never trust a cruise ship dentist with a paperclip-sealed glove.
7. If chaos clears a path through a casino, take the seat and spin
    the machine.
8. A good story beats a perfect reputation every time.
9. When strangers pull their chairs closer, you're doing
    something right.
10. If you're going to be trouble, at least be memorable trouble.
11. Storms will come. Hurricanes will come. Teeth will betray
    you.
    Cruise insurance is not optional.

12. If someone asks what you're doing with your life, tell them
    the truth:

    "I'm collecting stories."
13. Never assume you're the only one who nearly went under.
14. The most dangerous place in the world is a room where
    everyone is pretending to behave.
15. If the ocean gives you your voice back, use it.

THE "SCARLETT TROUBLE" COCKTAIL

For Book Clubs That Like Their Discussions Honest

Ingredients

- 1½ oz dark rum
- 1 oz cranberry juice
- ½ oz fresh lime juice
- Splash of pineapple juice
- Dash of bitters
- Ginger beer to top
- Lime wedge or cherry

Instructions

1. Fill a tall glass with ice.
2. Add rum, cranberry juice, lime juice, pineapple juice, and bitters.
3. Top with ginger beer.
4. Stir gently and garnish with lime or cherry.

Scarlett's serving advice:

"Drink responsibly… but tell your stories irresponsibly."

BOOK CLUB ICEBREAKER

Before starting the discussion, ask everyone:

"What is the most 'Scarlett' moment of your life?"

Examples might include:
    a)   A trip that went wildly wrong
    b)   A story that always gets laughs
    c)   A moment when chaos unexpectedly worked out
    d)   A time when you surprised yourself

It warms the room exactly the way Scarlett warms the smoking deck on the cruise ship.

SCARLETT'S GUIDE TO HOLDING A ROOM

*Lessons Learned Somewhere Between a
Cruise Deck and a Hurricane*

Scarlett didn't learn storytelling in a classroom.

She learned it in casinos, smoking sections, hurricanes, and rooms full of strangers who suddenly stopped leaving.

Here are the rules she discovered along the way.

1. Start With Something Small

You don't open with the craziest moment.

You start with something simple.

A cruise mishap.

A husband moment.

A bad decision that ended well.

If people laugh, you're in.

2. Watch the Lean

The moment people lean forward, you've got them.

That's when the story can stretch.

Pause.

Let the room breathe.

Then continue.

3. Tell the Truth… But Tell It Well

The best stories don't need exaggeration.

Real life is already outrageous.

Just give it rhythm.

4. Don't Rush the Punchline

Scarlett learned that the pause is half the story.

People laugh harder when they can see the trouble coming.

5. Make the Room Feel Included

The best storytellers don't perform at people.

They share with them.

That's why strangers pull their chairs closer.

6. Respect the Chaos

The moments that embarrass you today will become the stories people beg you to tell tomorrow.

Nothing is wasted.

7. Know When to Stop

Leave them wanting another story.

That's how you turn listeners into friends.

SCARLETT'S FINAL RULE

If people ask for another story…
Tell it.
If you ever find yourself sitting in a cruise ship smoking section and someone says,
"Tell the Manila one again" … pull up a chair.
You're about to hear a good story.

ABOUT THE AUTHOR

Scarlett grew up as a preacher's daughter but quickly discovered she had a talent for stirring just enough trouble to collect great stories.

Over the years she became a corporate rule-breaker, fearless traveler, and lifelong partner to her husband James, whose steady presence somehow survived decades of adventure.

After a stroke temporarily took away her voice, Scarlett found her way back through humor, storytelling, and an unexpected journey of recalibration.

She and James are now retired, still collecting stories wherever they go.

www.ingramcontent.com/pod-product-compliance
Lightning Source LLC
Chambersburg PA
CBHW021530150726
47990CB00006B/2170